Moose, Caribou and Reindeer

ALASKA GEOGRAPHIC.

Volume 23, Number 4

To teach many more to better know and more wisely use our natural resources...

EDITOR
Penny Rennick

PRODUCTION DIRECTOR
Kathy Doogan

MARKETING MANAGER
Pattey Parker Mancini

CIRCULATION/DATABASE MANAGER
Linda Flowers

EDITORIAL ASSISTANT
Kerre Martineau

BOARD OF DIRECTORS
Richard Carlson
Kathy Doogan
Penny Rennick

Robert A. Henning, **PRESIDENT EMERITUS**

POSTMASTER: Send address changes to:

ALASKA GEOGRAPHIC®
P.O. Box 93370
Anchorage, Alaska 99509-3370

PRINTED IN U.S.A.

ISBN: 1-56661-033-8

Price to non-members this issue: $19.95

COVER: *Muskoxen form a defensive perimeter to confront any intruder.* (Harry M. Walker)

PREVIOUS PAGE: *A bull caribou in his prime patrols the tundra near Wonder Lake in Denali National Park.* (Harry M. Walker)

OPPOSITE PAGE: *A bull moose makes a formidable adversary.* (Craig Brandt)

ALASKA GEOGRAPHIC® (ISSN 0361-1353) is published quarterly by The Alaska Geographic Society, 639 West International Airport Road, Unit 38, Anchorage, AK 99518. Periodicals postage paid at Anchorage, Alaska, and additional mailing offices. Copyright © 1997 by The Alaska Geographic Society. All rights reserved. Registered trademark: Alaska Geographic, ISSN 0361-1353; Key title Alaska Geographic.

THE ALASKA GEOGRAPHIC SOCIETY is a non-profit, educational organization dedicated to improving geographic understanding of Alaska and the North, putting geography back in the classroom and exploring new methods of teaching and learning.

MEMBERS RECEIVE *ALASKA GEOGRAPHIC*®, a high-quality, colorful quarterly that devotes each issue to monographic, in-depth coverage of a northern region or resource-oriented subject. Back issues are also available. For current membership rates, or to order or request a free catalog of back issues, contact: The Alaska Geographic Society, P.O. Box 93370, Anchorage, AK 99509-3370; phone (907) 562-0164, fax (907) 562-0479, e-mail: akgeo@aol.com

SUBMITTING PHOTOGRAPHS: Those interested in submitting photographs should write for a list of future topics or other specific photo needs and a copy of our editorial guidelines. We cannot be responsible for unsolicited submissions. Submissions not accompanied by sufficient postage for return by certified mail will be returned by regular mail.

CHANGE OF ADDRESS: The post office does not automatically forward *ALASKA GEOGRAPHIC*® when you move. To ensure continuous service, please notify us at least six weeks before moving. Send your new address and membership number or a mailing label from a recent *ALASKA GEOGRAPHIC*® to: The Alaska Geographic Society, Box 93370, Anchorage, AK 99509. If your book is returned to us by the post office, we will contact you to ask if you wish to receive a replacement for $5 (to cover postage costs).

COLOR SEPARATIONS:
Graphic Chromatics

PRINTING:
Hart Press

ABOUT THIS ISSUE: Anchorage resident Dick Emanuel wrote the article on moose for this issue and relied on Dr. Charles Schwartz of the Alaska Department of Fish and Game's Moose Research Center outside Soldotna and on Ed Crain of the Alaska Department of Fish and Game in Petersburg for information and/or review of the manuscript. For the article on caribou, *ALASKA GEOGRAPHIC*® turned to Jim Davis of Fairbanks, a nature photographer, writer, biologist and wildlife consultant formerly with the Alaska Department of Fish and Game. Jim thanks Alaska Department of Fish and Game staff Dan Reed, Larry Van Daele, Pat Valkenburg and Ken Whitten for providing information and for their help with the manuscript. Dr. Pam Groves of the University of Alaska Fairbanks' Institute of Arctic Biology wrote the article on muskox, a species with which she has worked for nearly 20 years. Kerre Martineau of *ALASKA GEOGRAPHIC*®'s editorial staff wrote the article on the Musk Ox Farm in Palmer and the text on the Large Animal Research Station in Fairbanks. *ALASKA GEOGRAPHIC*® thanks Geoff Carroll of the Alaska Department of Fish and Game in Barrow and Rich Harris of the National Park Service's Bering Land Bridge National Preserve staff in Nome for providing information on moose, caribou and muskox in their area.

The Library of Congress has cataloged this serial publication as follows:

Alaska Geographic. v.1-
    [Anchorage, Alaska Geographic Society] 1972-
    v. ill. (part col.). 23 x 31 cm.
    Quarterly
    Official publication of The Alaska Geographic Society.
    Key title: Alaska geographic, ISSN 0361-1353.

    1. Alaska—Description and travel—1959-
    —Periodicals. I. Alaska Geographic Society.

F901.A266   917.98'04'505   72-92087

Library of Congress   75[79112]   MARC-S.

Contents

Moose

By Richard P. Emanuel

Editor's note: *Dick Emanuel is a frequent contributor to* ALASKA GEOGRAPHIC® *and reports that he and his young daughter, Nicole, enjoyed watching a cow moose and twin calves make themselves at home in the yard of his Anchorage hillside home in spring 1996.*

The moose (*Alces alces*) has come to symbolize for many the spirit of the world's northern forests. Yet in some ways, it is a curious icon. With its large ears, enormous muzzle, massive hump, exceptionally long legs and unusual bell of hairy skin dangling from its throat, the moose is widely regarded as ungainly, even ugly. Strange associations for the largely unspoiled, lake-bejeweled northern forests that constitute moose country the world around.

In other respects, the mighty moose is a fitting symbol. Moose are the largest inhabitants of the vast forests they call home, slightly exceeding in size even Alaska's giant brown bears. The attributes that lead some to call moose ugly are in fact superb adaptations to the harsh, cold environment where they prevail. Large ears enable moose to detect predators like the wolf or bear. Their bulbous nose not only enhances a fine sense of smell, it also warms the subarctic air they inhale. Their long legs and muscular hump make movement through bogs or deep snow much easier. As for their bell, it puzzles scientists, but some believe it plays a role in the spectacular reproductive ritual known as rut.

There is another reason the moose is an apt symbol of the woods, at least in Alaska: A relative newcomer among Alaska mammals, the Alaska-Yukon subspecies of giant moose (*Alces alces gigas*) probably arrived from Siberia just as humans did. The route of Ice Age migration for both led across the Bering Land Bridge, exposed by fallen sea level when vast glaciers tied up much of the planet's fresh water. Glaciers advanced and retreated many times during the Pleistocene Epoch, between 1.8 million and 10,000 years ago, alternately exposing and inundating the bridge linking Siberia and Alaska. Well after the ice had begun its final retreat, sometime between 40,000 and 12,000 years ago, Ice Age men and modern moose probably ventured onto the land bridge. Indeed, the advance of the forest and the movement of game animals may have been the lures that led people into Alaska. Mankind and moose arrived

FACING PAGE: *A forkhorn bull challenges a mature adult in Denali National Park.* (Craig Brandt)

together and have shared Alaska's forests and tundra ever since.

Moose belong to the order *Artiodactyl*, or even-toed mammals, which includes sheep and cattle, pigs, hippos, camels and giraffes. Moose are ruminants, herbivores with four-chambered stomachs, two of which provide homes for symbiotic micro-organisms that digest cellulose. They are the largest living members of the deer family, the *Cervidae*, which includes more than 40 species worldwide. North American deer include caribou, mule deer, white-tailed deer and wapiti or American elk.

The terms moose and elk are, unfortunately, a source of some confusion worldwide. The European "elk" is in fact a subspecies of moose, *Alces alces*, while American elk or wapiti (*Cervus canadensis*) do not occur in Europe. When Europeans first encountered wapiti, they apparently mistook them for their own *Alces alces*, which they called elk. When they met American *Alces alces*, they adopted the Algonquin name for the beast, "moz" or "mons," which became "moose."

Today, moose range in a circumpolar

BELOW LEFT: *Long winters with deep snow cover present a hardship for many of Alaska's mammals, including moose. In 1990, severe winter weather caused many moose to starve and prompted a rescue attempt by the U.S. Army. Troops drove all-terrain vehicles into rural areas, in this case near Willow, to deliver fresh hay to starving moose. (Cary Anderson)*

BELOW: *A bull moose was resting near the divide at the head of the Resurrection River on the Kenai Peninsula when biologists overflew the animal. When the moose got to his feet, he cast his left antler and ran off. The biologists noted that the moose listed to his right and surmised that the animal's equilibrium had been thrown off with the dropping of the estimated 30 pounds of the left antler. (James L. Davis)*

belt of forest from Northern Europe and Asia across North America. Hunting and loss of woodland had extinguished moose from New England by the late 1800s, and similar pressures reduced their numbers in eastern Canada and the United States. Moose have recolonized much of their former range in North America, especially in New England and eastern Canada. They have expanded southward beyond their historic range into North Dakota, Colorado, Utah and Washington. Roughly a million moose live in North America today.

BELOW: *Hollow hairs aid flotation for this bull moose as it swims the wide Yukon River. (Steve McCutcheon)*

RIGHT: *Forty to 90 percent of young moose calves may not survive until their first autumn, falling victim to predators, drowning or other environmental factors. (Robin Brandt)*

Size

Depending on which biologist provides the information, moose are subdivided into six to eight subspecies, geographically or ecologically distinct groupings with slightly different characteristics. The Alaska-Yukon moose is the largest subspecies, while the Wyoming or Shiras moose, *A.a. shiras*, is among the smallest.

"Our Alaskan yearling is just about as large as the Shiras bull moose," says Chuck Schwartz, director of the

Moose Research Center of the Alaska Department of Fish and Game, outside Soldotna.

Alaska bull moose, or mature males, stand 6 to 7 feet tall at the shoulder and weigh 1,200 to 1,700 pounds. Cows, or mature females, weigh 800 to 1,200 pounds. In Alaska, the largest coastal brown bears and polar bears may approach a bull moose in size, but among land animals, only male bison, which may exceed 2,000 pounds, are bigger. Bison became extinct in

Alaska some 500 years ago, but 23 were reintroduced from Montana in 1928. Several hundred bison now reside in the state. Female bison are considerably smaller than males and weigh about the same as Alaska cow moose.

Tales of 2,000-pound moose are a myth, according to Schwartz. "I don't believe there are moose that weigh a ton," he says, "1,750 is probably a real bruiser." Schwartz personally helped document the biggest moose ever weighed. Bando, a bull at the Moose Research Center, rang up 1,693 pounds in his prime.

In addition to sheer size, bull moose are imposing for their antlers, the largest grown by any living animals. Antlers are bony growths sprouted on either side of the top of the skull. They may exceed 70 pounds and are shed and regrown each year. As in all other deer, with the exception of caribou, only male moose grow antlers.

Moose antlers have a striking shape that is usually described as palmate. Their form resembles an open hand, with a broad palm at the base from which fingers or tines extend. The record spread is 83 inches, or 1 inch short of 7 feet. They begin growing in April or May, nourished by a covering of velvety skin rich in blood vessels. During the summer months of growth, antlers are relatively soft and blood-engorged. In late summer, they begin to calcify and harden. As autumn nears and the rut begins, reproductive hormones reduce, then cut off the antlers' blood supply. The velvet skin dies, dries and is shed, revealing a shiny, hard rack ready for rut.

Antlers have a simple form in yearlings, usually a spike or a fork. Successive antlers become broader, more massive, with more tines each year. During a four-month growing season, a large rack may average a

FACING PAGE: *Ralph Mumm works to free a mired-down moose near Rock Lake on the Kenai Peninsula. (James L. Davis)*

RIGHT: *Bog areas are a particularly good habitat for spotting moose in summer. (Danny Daniels)*

A Denali National Park bull mounts a female during the mating season. Alaska-Yukon moose, unlike species of smaller moose, practice harem mating. A bull takes charge of a group of females and runs off any other males. He then closely shepherds his females to be available when they enter the 24-hour period when they are ready to mate. (Roy Corral)

half-pound of growth a day. Such antlers place tremendous nutritional and energy demands on a bull. As a bull enters old age, successive antlers grow smaller. A massive rack of antlers is thus the mark of a bull in his prime.

As an indicator of age and fitness, antlers serve to impress and attract females and to warn off rival bulls.

Antlers have a secondary function as weapons. While displays alone are often enough to establish dominance, bulls with nearly equal-size racks will combat to settle the issue of which gets to mate.

Breeding

Breeding behavior is one thing that sets Alaska-Yukon moose apart. In most subspecies, a bull will defend one or two cows at a time. The period of sexual readiness in a cow lasts only about 24 hours. A bull will court a cow nearing estrus for as long as a week, displaying and fighting off rivals until the cow is ready, or a bigger bull arrives. Having mated, the bull moves off in search of another willing cow. Such behavior is called paired mating.

Alaska-Yukon moose "generally breed in a harem arrangement," explains Schwartz. "One male will defend a group of females from other males, sometimes as many as 15 cows in a harem. He doesn't defend a territory because the group may move around. If he is strong enough and can defend that harem long enough, he may end up breeding with all of them."

The time of rut is a spectacular time to observe moose, if you are careful. Normally quite solitary, when leaves turn color and frost appears, moose begin to congregate in and around rutting arenas, relatively open areas where the animals can see one another.

BELOW: *Cow moose eat the placenta after giving birth to lessen the chances that predators will find their young. There are many hazards for young moose including brucellosis, a bacterial disease that primarily affects the reproductive and lymph systems. Left untreated, brucellosis can lead to debility and death. (Robin Brandt)*

RIGHT: *A cow encourages her newborn calf to stand. Moose calves can stand on wobbly legs within hours of birth. A cow's milk can be so rich that youngsters can gain 2 pounds a day. (Robin Brandt)*

ABOVE: *A newborn calf, less than 2 hours old, is unable to stand for any length of time. This calf's mother is nearby and will vigorously defend her offspring. (Nick Jans)*

RIGHT: *Cow moose usually bear a single calf, or twins if the habitat is particularly good. It is unusual to see a cow with triplets. (Steve McCutcheon)*

After feeding all summer, they are in peak condition. Mostly silent the rest of the year, moose during rut fill the woods with sound. Cows call to prospective mates with a high grunt or whine. Bulls emit a low, guttural call and thrash their racks against trees and shrubs, scraping off dangling shreds of velvet and polishing their antlers. The hollow sound of a large rack carries for miles, allowing other moose to size up potential mates or rivals.

Early in the courtship ritual, bulls dig rutting pits with their front hooves. Then they urinate in the pit, imparting a strong, musty odor believed to help bring cows into estrus. Cows are attracted to the bulls' "perfume" and may splash and roll in the urine-soaked mud. The bull splashes the mud on his antlers and on the bell or dewlap of loose skin on his throat. One function of the bell may be to catch this mud, Schwartz says. Cows often rub and caress the bull's head and

neck and sniff the musty bell.

From late September through early October, virtually all cows over 1 year of age will breed. Some yearling cows also breed, especially where food is plentiful. After about 230 days, cows give birth in late May or early June. They typically give birth to a single calf at the end of their first pregnancy, but twins are common in subsequent years and triplets are sometimes born. Calves weigh 25 to 30 pounds at birth but quickly gain weight, adding as

A bull in rut urinates to attract a cow. (Craig Brandt)

much as 2 pounds a day. They are weak initially and unable to stand but are on their feet within hours. Calves remain highly vulnerable to predators during their first summer.

Cows are very protective of calves and it is dangerous to come between mother and calf. Even yearlings are driven off by their mothers who fix their attention on newborns. Moose have few enemies to fear, but wolves and bears do pose a threat. A healthy adult moose is a formidable opponent, with front hooves able to trample and sometimes prevail over even a pack of wolves. Nevertheless, wolves and bears prey on moose with success and, especially during spring, calves may be an important part of their diet. Other than predation, the greatest threat to calves is probably drowning in swift-flowing streams. As a result of all hazards combined, according to Chuck Schwartz, between 40 and 90 percent of spring-born calves may be dead by autumn.

Diet

The Algonquin name for moose translates into English as "twig-eater," and the appellation fits. Moose are browsers, not grazers, subsisting chiefly on the twigs, leaves, buds and bark of shrubs and trees. "They eat very little

grass," says Schwartz. "Grass may make up 5 percent of their diet in spring or fall, when it's either very green and tender or there's not much else available."

Favored foods of moose depend upon where they live. Willows are popular with most moose. Alaska-Yukon moose rely on the leaves and twigs of willow, aspen and paper birch, according to

Schwartz. "Those three species are eaten both summer and winter," he says. "In summer, they strip the leaves off and eat primarily leaves. In fall and winter, they eat twigs. Fireweed is also an important summer food, as is *equisetum* or horsetail. Winter foods include lowbush cranberry, which is available only when there isn't much snow cover."

The woody browse that makes up the bulk of a moose's diet, particularly in fall and winter, generally lacks sodium and magnesium, electrolytes critical in many cellular functions. Aquatic plants, in contrast, may have 500 times the sodium content of terrestrial plants, and moose are commonly seen during summer wading chest-deep in ponds and lakes, munching mouthfuls of water lilies and pondweed with seeming relish.

Adult moose are quite at home in the water. They are excellent swimmers and cross small bodies of water readily and with ease. There are documented cases of moose diving as deep as 18 feet to reach aquatic plants. In addition to providing vital nutrients, water also affords a respite from the biting insects that plague moose and the summer heat that, with their insulating coats, they are ill-equipped to shed.

Where aquatic plants are scarce, moose may seek out mineral licks, areas with salty rock and soil rich in sodium and other minerals. To their peril and the detriment of motorists, moose are also attracted to road salt. Mixed with sand, the stuff is broadcast onto icy roads and winds up in ditches, where dark-colored moose are all but invisible, especially at night.

A black bear prepares to feed on a road-killed moose. (John L. Oldemeyer)

"We do have a significant road kill," says Schwartz. "We lose an average of about 225 moose a year on the Kenai Peninsula alone." Statewide, there are about 700 accidents involving moose in an average year. One or two motorists are killed, and many more suffer injury.

Whether they live near roads or in roadless areas, winter is a time of trial for moose. They generally enter autumn with up to 20 percent of their body in fat, only to find their favorite foods quickly disappearing with the frost and beneath the snow. Bull moose expend considerable energy during rut, but as they are preoccupied with tests of dominance and in mating, their appetite declines. Thus, their winter weight loss begins. A few months after rut, typically in December or January, bulls cast off their antlers, lightening their load a bit. The loss of antlers may also confer easier access to dense forests, where moose may go seeking food under reduced snow cover.

During the bountiful days of summer, a moose may consume more than 2.5 percent of its weight in dry browse each day. For an adult bull, that translates into 50 to 65 pounds of moist plant material, according to Schwartz. Most moose forage within a fairly restricted area called a home range, which rarely exceeds 15 square miles during the summer.

The lean times of winter may halve the amount of food a moose consumes, while it expands its home range to

BELOW: *Moose droppings, which some Alaskans dub "nuggets," reflect the animal's vegetarian diet. The pellets have generated much humor among Alaskans, who collect them to craft whimsical items such as swizzle sticks. (George Wuerthner)*

RIGHT: *Aquatic plants, including water lilies, provide much higher nutrition than do the tree bark and willow and alder twigs on which moose feed in winter. (Charles Schwartz)*

FACING PAGE: *Although government laws and officials encourage Alaskans to give moose a wide berth, pioneer Alaskans sometimes developed a close relationship with individual animals. In the early 1960s, Anchorage homesteader Mortimer "Moose" Moore had a tame moose. He also had bears. Moore was working with fish and game officials and had permission to keep the animals on his homestead at the northwest corner of Dowling and Lake Otis. (Steve McCutcheon)*

perhaps 20 square miles. The dry fare of winter actually alters a moose's droppings from summer's moist, pie-shaped deposits to winter's dry oval pellets with the texture of sawdust. These are the familiar "moose nuggets" sometimes varnished and sold as key-ring bobs or otherwise packaged by enterprising entrepreneurs. In Alaska, at least, the raw material is not lacking.

Calves, yearlings and past-prime bulls may enter winter in fine shape, but they do not have nearly the fat store available to adult cows. They may well starve if spring is slow in coming. Adult cows rarely starve except during unusually severe winters, according to Schwartz, who says that cows are "nearly immortal," easily living 12 to 14 years and occasionally

to age 20. Bulls over age 12 are rare.

Moose populations maintain a dynamic balance. They shift according to survival rates that respond to a winter's coldness and snow-cover, to predation and changing local forest conditions. "The real critical thing is winter forage," Schwartz observes. In Alaska, that means deciduous trees.

A forest fire may prove a boon to moose, if it is very hot. A hot fire burns down through the leaves, moss and other organic matter atop the soil. "Then you have a lot of reseeding of birch, willow and aspen, which is good for moose," explains Schwartz. "If you don't get a hot fire and get

down through the organic matter, the seedlings root in that organic layer, which tends to dry out, and the birch and willow seedlings don't survive."

A 1947 fire on the Kenai Peninsula scorched nearly 500 square miles and precipitated a moose explosion. A 1969

LEFT: *No telling what might pop up from a woodland pond. (William Wakeland)*

BELOW: *An aggregation of yearling moose forages in the Placer River valley on the Kenai Peninsula in late May. (James L. Davis)*

blaze on the northern Kenai Peninsula that consumed 135 square miles also boosted the moose population. This time the process was studied by scientists at the Moose Research Center.

"That was a very hot fire," says Schwartz, producing vigorous regrowth of deciduous trees. Concentrations of moose in the burned area rose from 1 or 2 per square mile before the fire to a peak of 15 or 16 per square mile.

"Five to 10 years after the burn, that's when it does a lot of good for moose," Schwartz explains. As the forest ages, young trees grow out of the reach of moose. Eventually, spruce begin to crowd out deciduous trees. "Twenty or 25 years after the fire, the quality of the habitat starts to decline."

Status and Distribution

Nature is always in flux. In Alaska, even the range of moose is in flux. The state is home to about 150,000 moose from Southeastern Alaska to the Arctic Slope.

In Southwestern Alaska, moose are following the slow spread of forest along the lower Yukon River. Fifty years ago, moose were unknown below Russian Mission. A 1985 count by the Alaska Department of Fish and Game turned up 400 to 500 moose in the 1,500-square-mile area between Russian Mission and Pilot Station. Today, the area supports more than 1,000 moose.

Prior to the 1940s, there were few moose north of the Brooks Range, but

about that time, enough migrated north to establish breeding populations on the Arctic Slope. From 1970 until 1991, Fish and Game surveys showed a stable number of moose in the area. Up to 1,600 animals browsed mostly in the willow-choked river valleys of the eastern slope. During the last five years, the area's moose population has crashed to about a third of its peak number. Calf mortality is nearly 100 percent, and in the summer of 1995, biologists found 18 mature moose dead in one river valley. Summer die-offs of

mature moose are almost unheard of, and scientists are scrambling for an answer. Overpopulation, harsh arctic winters, insect harassment, infectious disease and copper deficiency are all being considered. Perhaps a combination of factors is weakening the animals, leaving them more vulnerable to the hazards moose normally endure. Moose on the Arctic Slope are at the limit of their historic range, and their margin of survival is undoubtedly thin.

Moose in the 1970s also became abundant on the Seward Peninsula for the first time on record. Like their

cousins to the north, those populations have showed recent declines.

The moose story in Southeastern Alaska has some unusual twists. Moose are few or absent on most major islands in Southeast, just as they are absent from the Kodiak Islands, the Aleutians, the offshore islands of the Bering Sea and most islands in Prince William Sound. Moose are found, however, in the valley of the Stikine River, which flows from British Columbia to the Inside Passage, between Wrangell and Petersburg.

The Stikine animals are not Alaska-

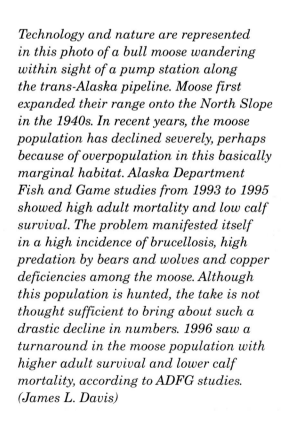

Technology and nature are represented in this photo of a bull moose wandering within sight of a pump station along the trans-Alaska pipeline. Moose first expanded their range onto the North Slope in the 1940s. In recent years, the moose population has declined severely, perhaps because of overpopulation in this basically marginal habitat. Alaska Department Fish and Game studies from 1993 to 1995 showed high adult mortality and low calf survival. The problem manifested itself in a high incidence of brucellosis, high predation by bears and wolves and copper deficiencies among the moose. Although this population is hunted, the take is not thought sufficient to bring about such a drastic decline in numbers. 1996 saw a turnaround in the moose population with higher adult survival and lower calf mortality, according to ADFG studies. (James L. Davis)

Moose browse in a stand of deciduous forest near Talkeetna in southcentral Alaska. (Corinne Smith)

Yukon moose, *Alces alces gigas*, according to Ed Crain of the Alaska Department of Fish and Game in Petersburg. They are *A.a. andersoni*, a subspecies common in British Columbia. Their ancestors migrated down the Stikine River valley long ago, for moose have been known in the area throughout historic time.

"They do have a different breeding style, they are pair breeders," Crain confirms.

The temperate rain forest of Southeast makes for a different diet, too. "There are willows but not that many, so the moose eat a lot of alder," Crain says. "They also eat hemlock, which is an evergreen, and they eat huckleberry. In winter, they tend to move into the old growth forest, where there's a lot less snow cover," thanks to the dense canopy overhead.

The number of Stikine moose rose in the 1970s, perhaps partly in response to regrowth in clear-cut areas. More recently, the population has dropped, Crain says. "The clear-cuts are getting pretty overgrown, so that habitat is declining." Hunting pressures have also stepped up, forcing tighter restrictions in recent years.

The most striking thing about Stikine moose is the prevalence of

abnormal antlers. "You see some real unusual antler formations," Crain says. "It's common to see some real oddballs. Things that look like the horns on an ox, things that go up and curve around in a strange way."

Crain speculates that these curiosities may result from some combination of three factors: inbreeding, malnutrition due to poor soils depleted by the region's tremendous rainfall, and damage to growing antlers sustained in the unusually dense forest.

Urban Moose

If moose are widely felt to embody the spirit of the world's boreal forests, not all are creatures of the far-off wilds. There are urban moose as well, about 2,000 within the sprawling Municipality of Anchorage. As many as 800 moose may dwell in the Anchorage bowl, bounded by the Chugach Mountains and the two arms of Cook Inlet, an area home to about 250,000 people. Most urban moose are inoffensive brutes, with a live-and-let-live attitude. But they are still wild animals that may weigh more than 1,000 pounds.

The most serious problem with urban moose is traffic. Accidents in

Anchorage kill about 100 moose a year and pose a serious threat to motorists. The danger is greatest during winter months when long nights cloak the creatures just when high snowfall in the mountains may force them to forage in the populous lowlands.

In addition to roads, interactions between people and moose are common on the paved paths where Anchorageites bicycle, jog, ski or walk, often with their children. Popular sections of these paths wind along greenbelts lined with willows, birch and cottonwoods guarding creeks that conduct snow melt from the mountains. Moose have browsed these waterways and adjacent areas for centuries and see no reason they can't accommodate a few people. Most of the time.

In October 1993, a moose trampled a 66-year old woman to death in her Anchorage backyard. She suffered head injuries, perhaps sustained when she got between her dog and an angry moose.

In January 1995, an elderly man was killed by a moose on the campus of the University of Alaska in Anchorage. The cow and her calf had reportedly been

ABOVE: *A moose takes to the depths of Clearwater Lake near Delta Junction to escape harassing flies. (James L. Davis)*

RIGHT: *Moose epitomize the northern forest. The Alaska-Yukon subspecies of moose is the largest member of the world's deer family. (Chlaus Lotscher)*

taunted by students and pelted with snowballs over the preceding days. After an altercation with a professor a few days later, the cow was shot by officials.

It is safe to say that the overwhelming majority of encounters with moose in Anchorage are happy. Most people are pleased to live in a city close enough to nature to bestow visits by half-ton wild herbivores. For their part, the moose enjoy munching on mountain ash and other ornamental trees and shrubs, not to mention the occasional cabbage or broccoli proffered by helpful gardeners.

True, moose can make short work of a labor-intensive garden or inflict serious damage on expensively landscaped lots. But most people, once a little time has dimmed the memory

A bull moose with water dripping from his shedding velvet provides comic relief on a visit to Denali National Park. (Harry M. Walker)

of the loss, are philosophical about the price they pay to live with moose.

Still, despite their usual indifference to humanity, urban moose remain untamed — and unpredictable. People who forget this court disaster, for themselves and for moose. In Alaska, it is illegal as well as dangerous to feed moose, punishable by a fine of up to $5,000 and up to a year in jail. A moose who is fed by people may come to associate humans with food and may grow aggressive in demanding more from the next person he meets. Such an animal is bound to run afoul of humanity and will likely wind up being killed.

People across Alaska, from Anchorage and Fairbanks to smaller communities to isolated cabins, share their woodlands with moose. A wise person respects moose, gives ground to one met in the woods, on a roadway or path, observes from a distance, on a deck or through a window. Millennia ago, as the glaciers receded, moose and humans arrived in Alaska. Our ancestors shared the forests with their ancestors. Alaskans today are privileged to share their homes with such wild creatures. Or is it we who share their homes? ∎

Caribou

By James L. Davis

Editor's note: *Jim retired from the Alaska Department of Fish and Game after spending most of the 1970s and 1980s specializing in caribou research and management. He now works in nature photography, free-lance writing and wildlife consulting.*

Jim thanks the following Alaska Department of Fish and Game staff for providing published and unpublished information and for their general helpfulness: Dan Reed, Larry Van Daele, Pat Valkenburg and Ken Whitten.

Introduction

What spectacles must have been seared into the memories of those early Americans privileged to witness the massing of the bison on the plains, the incredible roosts of the passenger pigeons, or the sky-darkening flights of waterfowl. Sadly, those aggregations of wildlife have vanished.

But even today, assemblages of caribou can and do still stagger the imagination and enrich our human experience. Each year in late June and early July, the bulk of large Alaska caribou herds, like the Western Arctic (currently numbering nearly half a million), Porcupine, Mulchatna, and Nelchina gather in dense post-calving aggregations. More such herds aggregate in Canada: the Bluenose, Bathurst, Beverly, Kaminuriak and George River herds. These ephemeral aggregations can reach densities of many thousands per square mile and are without rival as the greatest gathering of land mammals in the Americas.

For 40 years I have oriented my life, both vocationally and avocationally, to maximize encounters with wildlife. My experiences with caribou aggregations rank among my best. Imagine my first encounter with the Western Arctic herd in early October 1974. Flying in a Helio-Courier airplane with bush pilot Nelson Walker from Kotzebue and fellow wildlife biologist Carl Grauvogel, we encountered migrating caribou traveling south along the coast near the mouth of the Noatak River. The migration consisted of a nose-to-tail single-file chain of caribou with few breaks between animals. The migration stretched north to Cape Thompson, a distance exceeding 100 air miles. Carl and I each counted more than 60,000 caribou and our counts only differed by about 200. Many times since then I have seen post-calving aggregations containing several times that many

FACING PAGE: *Fall brings the breeding season, when bulls compete with one another for the opportunity to mate with the females. (Craig Brandt)*

caribou in just a few square miles. These aggregations remind me of a swarm of bees coming together, spreading out, splitting into smaller groups, re-aggregating and eventually dispersing. What the bee swarm does in minutes occurs during a couple of weeks in the caribou.

Nomenclature

All reindeer and caribou belong to the genus *Rangifer* and the species *tarandus*. All scientific names contained in the literature for the various subspecies combined with all common names used by the culturally diverse human inhabitants of the caribou's range would create an impressively long list.

In North America, most people call all wild members of *Rangifer tarandus* caribou and their domestic "cousins" reindeer. (Reindeer first came to Alaska as imports from Siberia in the late 1800s.) Eurasians favor the terms wild and domestic reindeer. *Rangifer* commonly refers to any one or combination of the above.

Northern Canadians still call caribou "deer" or more commonly "the deer."

The word caribou apparently derived from the Micmac Indian name for the animal *xalibu*, which means "the pawer." This fits the caribou well based on the animal's habit of pawing through snow (cratering) for its winter forage. The French *carre-boeuf* is another possible origin, but its meaning, "four-horned ox" isn't particularly apt.

Indians and Eskimos have varied names for the caribou. Eskimos use the words *tuktu, tuktuk, tuttu* or *tuntu* with various spellings in referring to caribou of unspecified age and sex. Eskimos also have specific names for individual caribou, including *pagniq* (adult bull), *julavak* (adult female) and *norraq* (calf). Some common Indian words for caribou include the following: *et-then* (Chippewan), *eh-tik* (Cree), *ek-wo-wetsi* (Dogrib), *no-ti* (Slave) and *anaay* (Athabaskan, Ahtna). Aleuts use the word *itxayax* for caribou.

At present most authorities recognize four subspecies of caribou in North America and a fifth, formerly of the Queen Charlotte Islands, British Columbia, is extinct. A sixth subspecies occurs in Greenland. Nomenclature follows: *Rangifer tarandus groenlandicus*, barren-ground caribou; *R. t. granti*, Alaskan barren-ground caribou; *R. t. caribou*, woodland caribou; *R. t. pearyi*, Peary caribou; *R. t. dawsoni* (extinct); and *R. t. eogroenlandicus*, Greenland caribou.

The Boone and Crockett Club includes a mountain caribou category for caribou trophy classification for caribou from northern British Columbia, and parts of the Yukon and Northwest Territories.

All past taxonomy of caribou has relied on the traditional methods heavily dependent on skull and skeleton characteristics. It will be enlightening to see future revisions for *Rangifer* based on new genetic-based techniques using DNA.

History of the Species

Like many other mammals present in today's arctic taiga and tundra

ABOVE LEFT: *Bull caribou seek respite from tourists in a protected area adjacent to the Eielson Visitor Center at Denali National Park. (Roy Corral)*

ABOVE: *By winter the rut is over, and caribou concentrate on finding food and shelter to survive the season. (Craig Brandt)*

animal communities, caribou are survivors from the Pleistocene. Other Pleistocene survivors familiar to the caribou include the bison, moose, elk, wolf, brown/grizzly bear, squirrels, lemmings, foxes and voles.

Caribou have probably roamed the North for more than 1 million years, although the earliest evidence dates back only 440,000 years and comes from central Germany. Evidence suggests a Eurasian origin for *Rangifer*.

Apparently caribou reached at least as far east as Alaska before the Penultimate Glaciation, perhaps 100,000 years ago, and remained in North America continuously since that time. During the Wisconsin Glaciation, about 10,000 to 70,000 years ago, caribou occurred in the Alaska-Yukon Refugium and throughout the belt of tundra occurring along the edge of the ice sheet from New Jersey to the mountainous region of the Southwest in present-day New Mexico to Nevada. Caribou probably also extended southward into forested regions as they do today. After the last glaciation, caribou undoubtedly followed the retreating ice to the localities where present-day populations are found.

Description

Being even-toed ruminants with four-compartment stomachs, caribou fall into the order *Artiodactyl* and the deer family, *Cervidae*. Antlers on both sexes, well-marked tarsal (lower leg) and interdigital (between the hooves) glands, and relatively simple crests on the cheek teeth all suggest the primitive nature of *Rangifer* compared to other deer.

Caribou have relatively long legs, large hooves and broad muzzles. They have elongated heads, with straight forehead-nose profiles in females and young males and "Roman noses" on many mature males. Except in Peary caribou, they have a blunt muzzle, well-haired other than the small oval at the tip of the nose. The physical appearances of caribou differ slightly among subspecies.

Being precocial, caribou calves can

In winter, caribou seek areas of shallow snow, but they are adept at finding food under deep, soft snow. This member of the Western Arctic herd forages in late April in northwestern Alaska. (James L. Davis)

follow their mothers within one hour of birth. This early mobility reduces their vulnerability to predation on the open tundra.

In Alaska herds, 97 to 99 percent of females have antlers, but many females in Ontario, Quebec and Newfoundland are bald, up to 95 percent in one Newfoundland herd.

Antler size and form shows great sexual dimorphism. Males sport large, showy antlers, often with several dozen points. Brow tines, the lowest points, form palmate and vertically oriented structures called shovels. Horizontally oriented bez tines, sometimes partially palmate, fork from the main beams just above the brow tines.

Caribou exhibit a more compressed breeding period than other deer. Most breed in a one-week period in the middle or end of October depending upon the specific herd. Females who fail to conceive can experience recurrent heat periods at intervals of 10 to 12 days. The gestation period is about 228 days. Twinning is rare and puberty is most often reached at 29 months; however, in high-quality populations, puberty is common at 17 months. Males are probably physiologically capable of breeding at these corresponding ages, but are behaviorally restricted by older

Predators and prey meet in Denali National Park. As of 1995, more than 2,000 caribou roamed the park. (Harry M. Walker)

bulls. Few cows live past 16 years and few males past 12, but apparently both sexes remain reproductively active. In most herds, cows give birth in May or early June. About 90 percent of births occur during a 10-day period. Dates of breeding and parturition vary among herds, but vary only slightly within herds if environmental and nutritional conditions remain similar over time. Nutritional condition of the cows can, to some degree, affect the gestation

period; poor nutrition seems to retard fetal development in the third trimester and lengthens gestation.

Size

Caribou average larger in size and weight than mule deer but smaller than elk. In general, mature female caribou average about 10 to 15 percent smaller in skeleton size and weigh 10 to 50 percent less than adult males. Seasonal differences in body weights can vary

Two cows and a calf pause along one of the many elevated gravel roads that crisscross the Prudhoe Bay oilfields. Caribou sometimes use the roads to get up into the wind and gain relief from swarming insects. (Jay Schauer)

Males weigh about 240 pounds for Peary caribou.

Calves weigh from 11 to 20 pounds at birth, but grow rapidly and can gain almost 1 pound per day for the first 100 days of life.

Pelage

At birth calves have a light brown or red brown body and a dark brown to black dorsal stripe from the neck to the tail. Their undersides are white or light gray.

Subspecies differ regarding color of pelage as do individuals within subspecies. Some animals are clove brown or various shades of gray. Lighter underparts and white leg socks characterize caribou. Flank stripes vary from prominent to lacking. The forest-dwelling woodland caribou have the darkest pelage and Peary caribou the lightest, with more gray than brown in their coats.

Each spring caribou shed their winter pelage, which often falls out in patches. Hair is so easily rubbed from caribou at this time that biologists have to be careful when handling caribou to prevent partially denuding them.

greatly in both males and females. Males can lose 25 percent of their weight during the autumn rut, as do females during some winters.

Average weights differ among the various subspecies, geographically within subspecies, and even within the same herd over time if population size or environmental conditions vary. Males of the larger subspecies, like those in Alaska south of the Brooks Range, northern British Columbia and Quebec/Labrador, weigh about 400 to 600 pounds and females about 200 to 300 pounds. Barren-ground caribou of the central Canadian mainland and those of Northern Yukon and Alaska's Arctic Slope weigh about 275 to 375 pounds for adult males and 200 pounds for females.

Caribou have an acute sense of smell and can locate food under deep snow by smell. Caribou seem to rely on their senses more when alone or gathered in small groups. As they come together in large aggregations, group dynamics seem to influence their behavior more than particular senses. (Harry M. Walker)

Very dark new hair underneath contributes to a ragged appearance for a short time. Adult bulls develop sleek summer coats first, followed by subadults, yearlings, cows without calves, and last, by maternal cows. By August most caribou have dark, short-haired new coats. By late August and early September, the hair lightens and longer, white-tipped guard hairs grow to form the winter coat. By late September, the bulls have developed handsome white neck manes much more pronounced than on females. The pelage now shows the maximum contrast in coloration. During winter, the guard hairs become bleached over time and many hair tips break off, resulting in a general lightening and loss of color contrast.

The Senses

In my experience, single caribou and those in small groups respond to their senses more than caribou in large groups. The senses of sight, smell and hearing seem more or less inactive as warning agents when the animals mass in groups at certain seasons. Caribou in large herds often appear indifferent to man's presence. I have commonly landed small aircraft beside large groups of caribou, with individuals showing little or no reaction. To be sure, huge differences exist in the reaction of caribou to the presence and sound of mechanized vehicles. Differences come from the composition of the groups, the time of year, and the caribou's past experience. Bulls and cows without young calves react least. Huge between-herd differences exist; herds targeted by snow machine hunters often stampede wildly at the sound of motors in the absence of dense cover or other escape habitat. Of the herds I studied in Alaska, the Western Arctic reacted most to engine noise and Delta reacted least.

Occasionally, individual caribou appear to have one or more senses dulled or inactive under certain circumstances like the stress of fly season. Caribou sometimes sleep so deeply that they appear comatose. For example, seeing an apparently dead calf floating down a river on an ice pan, men canoed out to salvage it

before it reached loudly thundering rapids less than 200 yards away. When they reached the ice, amazingly, the calf leapt to its feet and swam ashore. More than once I have landed a ski-equipped aircraft on a lake and glided up to an apparently dead animal, only to see it awake startled and surprised at the intrusion. Likewise I've landed in a helicopter only yards away before sleeping

caribou showed any sign of life.

In my experience, caribou rely most on their sense of smell. Anecdotes tell of scenting humans up to a mile away. Canadian Indians believe that caribou change migration routes to wintering areas if summer forest fires occur on the forested winter ranges. They believe that the caribou smell the smoke and know what areas to avoid even though they are hundreds of miles north during the time of the fires. For sure caribou have an unerring ability to scent food under deep snow. However, caribou frequently appear to doubt the evidence presented by their sense of smell. Even at close range to humans, caribou often return downwind again and again, or even come closer after their initial alarm, as if to confirm by sight what their sense of smell had told them. Or perhaps they are just curious. But, conversely, caribou frequently return downwind to confirm by smell

LEFT: *A caribou bull from the Western Arctic herd is being fitted with a radio collar at Onion Portage on the Kobuk River. State biologists use radio- and satellite-tracking devices to study the migration pattern of the herd. (Nick Jans)*

FACING PAGE: *Caribou from the Western Arctic herd cross the Kobuk River in August. A coat of hollow hairs increases buoyancy, enabling caribou to swim for some distance with ease. (Nick Jans)*

Members of Alaska's largest caribou herd migrate between the Seward Peninsula and Selawik Lowlands north to the North Slope in one of the continent's grandest wildlife spectacles. This segment of the Western Arctic herd is crossing the Kukpuk River in the DeLong Mountains inland from Point Hope. (James L. Davis)

what their vision first allowed them to detect.

The caribou's sense of hearing seems less efficient than its sense of smell. Some observers speculate that this can be attributed to the small size of the external ear as compared with ears of other deer. Many people who encounter caribou in open habitat infer that they do not have acute hearing or at least pay little attention to sound. Hearing alone seldom triggers the flight reflex. However, from hunting and stalking caribou during winter in wooded habitat, I know that caribou have a keen sense of hearing, and rely heavily on it to first alert them to danger, particularly if wolves have been present. Once alerted they then employ their sight and smell to help them decipher the presence of man, predators or non-threatening animals.

Caribou sometimes completely ignore loud, extraneous noises. Several times I have fired a rifle within a hundred yards of caribou, and sometimes they did not even turn their heads to face the direction of the noise. The same is true of rocks falling. Caribou show great variation to hearing nearby howling wolves: sometimes indifference and sometimes intense concern. Once when trying to determine the ratio of newborn calves to cows, I had watched caribou for hours feeding in brush that largely obscured them and I was running out of time. I howled like a wolf, and immediately the cows gathered up their calves, coalesced and moved into lower vegetation where visibility was improved. Aircraft noise appears to stimulate alarm only at short ranges. Some people attribute the success of open approaches, or of hunting in coarse camouflage, to the lack of attention to noises. I know several people who have stalked up to unobservant caribou and startled them with a touch.

The caribou's eyes have little sensitivity to color and form and serve poorly as an initial warning agent. Frequently, feeding or migrating caribou have walked within a few feet of me, while I remained motionless and downwind; even though I was within plain sight. Caribou apparently recognize a motionless man as something to be walked around, but they do not necessarily associate him with danger. They react similarly to a

A caribou bull munches on a willow shrub. Caribou eat a variety of lichens and seed plants with a marked preference for vascular plants and mushrooms in summer. In winter, they graze on lichens, and dig for green forage such as sedges and leaves of evergreen shrubs. (Harry M. Walker)

freshly killed caribou; they will detour around the body at less than 10 feet.

Though insensitive to color and form, they can detect movement remarkably. Many times caribou have foiled my stalks for hunting or observation by spotting me as I moved, often at distances approaching a mile, even though I wore camouflaged clothing. Sometimes this attention to movement makes caribou hunting difficult in the presence of open snow backgrounds or in tundra areas.

Caribou exhibit a well-defined sense of taste, and perhaps touch as well, as they feed. They selectively choose foods at all seasons, but particularly during winter.

Caribou are mostly silent, except for some weeks after calving and during the rut. Cows and calves communicate with short grunts, trying to maintain contact in moving herds. Occasionally startled males and females make a sharp snort, which may be involuntary. During the rut, caribou bulls make grunting sounds and another sound, a snoring bellowing, by quickly inhaling and exhaling.

A characteristic clicking noise emanates from the hooves of caribou and reindeer whenever they move. The first explanation that comes to mind is that the two individual hooves on each foot must be clicking together, but that is not the explanation. The noise comes from the displacement of muscle tendons, interplay of carpal or sesamoid bones (the small bones of the foot) and the cohesion between various tissue layers.

Cold Adaptations

In caribou, as in all mammals that do not hibernate, body temperature is constant and vital. Animals have two ways of coping with cold: They can increase their metabolic rate (their internal heat production) by eating large amounts of food, and they can prevent loss of body heat through conservation of energy and heat. Caribou strongly orient toward the latter approach. In fact, caribou, like

By mid-October, adult bulls from the Denali herd sport their prime coat as they forage among the foothills of the Alaska Range. (James L. Davis)

most deer living in temperate climates, reduce their basic metabolic rate in winter.

Fat and hair insulate caribou from the cold and enable them to live in the Arctic. To prevent excessive heat loss from their long legs, caribou maintain two internal temperatures: a body temperature of near 105 degrees F and a 50-degrees-cooler leg temperature. Routed like two cables in a conduit, the outflowing blood in the arteries transmits its warmth to the chilled venous blood returning from the legs. Constriction of blood vessels in the extremities permits blood flow just sufficient to prevent frost damage, and simultaneously ensures little loss of precious body heat to the cold ambient air.

Caribou are so well-adapted to their northern environment that some scientists call them chionophiles (snow lovers). The caribou's long guard hairs contain many air cells, and being thicker at the tip than at the base, they appear club-shaped. This, coupled with the caribou's ability to contract their skin to pack the hairs, creates tiny air spaces near the skin. In addition, caribou have a fine underwool near the bases of the guard

hairs. This combination makes the caribou nearly "winter proof."

Distribution and Status: Past and Present

Caribou and Eurasian wild reindeer are distributed throughout much of the Arctic and collectively comprise the specie's Holarctic distribution. The wild reindeer occurring in Northern Europe and Asia constitute the specie's Palearctic distribution. And the caribou's Nearctic distribution

refers to its North American distribution throughout Canada and Alaska's tundra and taiga biomes, including Greenland.

The barren-ground subspecies of the Nearctic occurs throughout Baffin Island, Coats Island, Ungava, portions of northern Ontario, northwestern Yukon, the districts of Mackenzie and Keewatin in Northwest Territories, the northern portions of the three Prairie Provinces and much of Alaska excluding Southeast.

The woodland caribou's distribution has decreased considerably since the 1800s. Factors involved in the decline have been the loss and change of habitat due to destruction of climax forests, overhunting and the change of predator/prey communities where the addition of moose and deer have introduced alternate prey into once-simpler wolf, bear, caribou systems. In addition white-tailed deer are carriers of "moose sickness," a parasitic brain worm that can prove fatal to caribou.

The woodland subspecies occupies the boreal forest and alpine tundra extensions of suitable mountainous habitats. Woodland caribou once occurred in Maine, New Hampshire, Vermont, Michigan, Minnesota, New Brunswick, Nova Scotia and Prince Edward Island. In eastern North America, the woodland caribou have now become limited to Newfoundland, Quebec, north of the St. Lawrence River, and Ontario. To the west they occur in Manitoba, Saskatchewan, Alberta, British Columbia, and north into the District of Mackenzie, Northwest Territories, and the Yukon.

Until just the past few years, a remnant population occurred in northern Idaho, northeast Washington, northwestern Montana and adjacent British Columbia. This endangered population now occurs only in Idaho and British Columbia. In recent years, caribou from farther north in B. C. have been transplanted into this area to augment the remnant population. And just this year caribou were reintroduced to Washington.

Peary caribou have ranged as far south as the mainland coast of the Arctic Ocean, and, in the past, have intermixed with barren-ground caribou from the Canadian mainland. Mainland barren-ground caribou have in the past migrated north to the more southerly islands of the Arctic Archipelago and shared portions of summer ranges. Most of this intermixing ceased by the 1930s.

Numbers

Currently, Alaska has considerably more caribou than people: about 1 million caribou versus half that number of humans. The Alaska Department of Fish and Game estimates that about 960,000 caribou resided in Alaska during 1996. These caribou occur in 31

A bull from the Delta herd displays rutting behavior around an estrous female. (James L. Davis)

more-or-less distinct subpopulations or herds (see Table I at right).

Biologists have named most of the major caribou herds after the geographical locations of their calving grounds. Biologists define a herd of caribou as being those caribou who for two or more years share a common calving ground. Four of Alaska's herds fail to recognize one of mankind's great inventions, the U.S./Canada border. Caribou from the Chisana, Fortymile, Porcupine and in recent years even the Nelchina herds have crossed the border annually, spending portions of the year in Canada.

Herd size ranges from as few as 50 to 90 in the Twin Lakes, Fox River and Kenai Lowlands herds to 450,000 in the Western Arctic herd. Other large herds are the Mulchatna (200,000), Porcupine (152,000) and Nelchina (50,000).

Of Alaska's current 31 caribou herds, six began as transplants from other herds. The Adak, Kenai Mountains and Kenai Lowlands herds have descended from transplants from the Nelchina herd in the 1960s. Two additional herds on the Kenai Peninsula, the Fox River and Killey River herds, arose from transplants made in the 1980s, again from the Nelchina herd. The largest transplanted herd in Alaska, the Nushagak Peninsula herd (1,500 in 1996) originated as a 1988 transplant from the Northern Alaska Peninsula herd.

We can only guess regarding how

Table I: Alaska Caribou Herds in 1995

MAP NUMBER /HERD	POPULATION SIZE	MAP NUMBER /HERD	POPULATION SIZE
1 Adak	1,500	18 Mulchatna	200,000
2 Andreafsky	Possibly extinct	19 Nelchina	50,281
3 Beaver Mountains	500	20 Northern Alaska Peninsula	12,000
4 Central Arctic	18,100	21 Nushagak Peninsula	1,519
5 Chisana	775	22 Porcupine	152,000
6 Delta	4,700	23 Rainy Pass	500?
7 Denali	2,300	24 Ray Mountains	1,750
8 Farewell-Big River	750	25 Southern Alaska Peninsula	1,550
9 Fortymile	22,600	26 Sunshine Mountains	600
10 Fox River	85	27 Teshekpuk	27,630
11 Galena Mountain	400	28 Tonzona	800
12 Kenai Lowlands	90	29 Twin Lakes	50
13 Kenai Mountains	425	30 Western Arctic	450,000
14 Killey River	290	31 White Mountains	1,200
15 Kilbuck	4,216	32 Wolf Mountain	625
16 Macomb	500	33 Yanert	(not distinguishable from Delta Herd since 1987)
17 Mentasta	852		

(Source: Alaska Department of Fish and Game, Fairbanks)

Location of Alaskan Caribou Herds

many caribou were originally in North America. But undoubtedly the numbers fluctuated considerably throughout time. Some biologists estimate that perhaps 2 million caribou resided in Alaska, with another 3 million to 4 million living in Canada.

Mortality and Welfare Factors: Mortality Factors

Caribou calves die from a multitude of factors, including birth defects, accidents, social interactions such as trampling, windchill, desertion and predation. An abundance of wolves and grizzly bears can contribute to calf mortality during the first year exceeding 80 percent. Several Alaska herds that I studied dropped from almost 90 calves per 100 cows at the end of calving to less than 5 calves per 100 cows by fall.

Following hard winters, pregnant females weigh less and produce smaller calves. These small calves are less viable and more susceptible to mortality from harsh weather. Desertion can be a significant cause of death under some circumstances. When we handled calves for scientific study, the cows with high nutritional status more aggressively defended their calves from us than did those with lower nutritional status.

Death among adults results from drowning, social interactions during breeding, death in parturition, disease, predation and starvation.

From 1972 to 1974 a large portion of the Peary caribou population died. The population on 20 islands numbered 24,320 in 1961, but in 1974, only 2,676 caribou remained. This die-off resulted because snow and/or ice prevented the animals from reaching food.

Hunting

The historic and current vital importance of caribou to northern people, both native and non-Native, has been documented by explorers,

anthropologists, archaeologists and wildlife biologists. To many Natives, the caribou once meant life. They ate its meat, dressed in its fur and made shelters from its hides. From its antlers and bones, they made tools, toys and weapons.

Northern peoples no longer depend exclusively on hunting, but caribou meat still provides an important and highly valued source of food in many communities, and the people, particularly Natives, consider the right to hunt a basic part of their cultural identity.

Currently, several individual herds of caribou in Alaska and Canada are numerically depressed. However, the general trend in the 1980s and 1990s has been major overall population growth. This has temporarily lessened concerns about overhunting. But it would be folly to forget the lessons of history.

Repeatedly, caribou numbers have declined by uncurbed and excessive hunting. In just 10 years, between 1965 and 1975, Alaska lost more than half its caribou with overhunting playing a significant role. Such declines have occurred recurrently in both Canada and Alaska ever since widely dispersed trapper-prospector populations arrived and Indians and Eskimos obtained general access to modern firearms and ammunition.

Intermittently, the chance to profit from killing caribou has accelerated their harvest. Around the turn of this century, market hunting for meat and heads contributed to declines and local extinctions. More recently, antler prices have become high enough to induce some hunting for antler harvest alone.

However, as noted in 1986 by Fred Bruemmer in *Arctic Animals*: "Infinitely more serious than such odd and incidental stimuli to increased hunting of certain arctic animals are three factors that will determine the future of arctic wildlife: widespread industrial

This calf from the Delta herd is just a few hours old. Calves weigh from 11 to 20 pounds at birth, but gain weight quickly, as much as 1 pound daily, for the first 100 days of their life. (James L. Davis)

exploration and exploitation of the North's mineral resources; the natives' insistence on hunting, preferably without limitations, as their birthright and as the sine qua non of their cultural survival; and a philosophy that views animals primarily in terms of their potential monetary value.

"The natives of the North argue with great cogency that it is their land, that whites have been largely responsible for the initial decimation of arctic wildlife, and that hunting is an integral and essential part of their way of life. While justified, these arguments skirt the fact that northern animal resources are limited, that human populations in the North are rapidly increasing, and that snowmobiles, high-powered rifles, speedboats, and even aircraft now make hunting so efficient that without some controls the most avidly hunted species, such as the caribou, are bound to decline. It is probable that only a deep involvement of the native people in the process of protection and perpetuation of arctic wildlife will halt and perhaps even reverse this fatal trend."

In this regard government agencies in both Canada and Alaska are

currently involved in co-management of wildlife with various Native groups.

Insect Pests

If anyone wants to really understand the caribou's life, they have to see firsthand the torture that the summer hordes of arctic insects inflict on them. Insect torment of caribou comes close to "hell on earth." I had to witness this to

believe it. I was a "doubting Thomas" when I read about how adversely insects affect caribou. Earlier I had read the same about elk, but when I began studying them in Idaho, my studies showed that elk and mosquitoes were most abundant when quantity and quality of forage offered optimum nutrition for the elk. I expected something similar when I began

A caribou crosses Arrigetch Creek during the fall migration through Gates of the Arctic National Park in the Brooks Range. Drowning causes some mortality, even among adult caribou. (Chlaus Lotscher)

FACING PAGE: *Members of the Porcupine herd seek shelter from pesky insects on the shorefast ice of Beaufort Lagoon along the shore of the Arctic National Wildlife Refuge. (James L. Davis)*

RIGHT: *Thimble-sized warble fly larvae account for the "blotches" along the back of this female on the North Slope. A succession of insect species — mosquitoes, warble and bot flies — torment the caribou from spring until fall's frost. Weak, malnourished animals can fall victim to this pestilent onslaught. (James L. Davis)*

studying caribou. However, I was convinced quickly that caribou go to great lengths to avoid or lessen their exposure to insects, including foregoing optimum foraging.

The first insect harassment each spring comes from mosquitoes. Concurrent with the birthing of caribou calves, mosquitoes emerge from the tundra's abundant water pools. In apparent response to these insect hordes, the widely scattered caribou coalesce into increasingly larger groups until the famous post-calving aggregations exist. Caribou aggregate so close together that mosquitoes must hover above them.

Just as the mosquitoes start to thin out, warble and bot flies besiege the caribou. Both flies look like slender, small, hairy bees, and their insistent buzzing drives the caribou wild and

pushes them to exhaustion. Warble flies lay their eggs on the hair of legs and abdomen of caribou. The larvae hatch, bore through the skin, burrow upwards and lodge beneath the hide on the rump and back. The literature reports that some caribou host more than 1,000 of these thimble-sized maggots. A co-worker and I counted nearly 2,000 in each of several emaciated yearling caribou that died of malnutrition in late winter, perhaps because of the heavy parasite burden.

The viviparous bot flies deposit their larvae in the caribou's nostrils. The

larvae then migrate to the throat. Victims shiver and shake violently to dislodge the warble flies, or race frantically to escape them. And they stand, wild-eyed and distraught, with muzzles close to the ground, trying to avoid the pesky bot flies. Despite these avoidance tactics, nearly all caribou are infested with these parasites.

To reduce insect attacks, caribou seek hilltops with strong winds, snow and ice fields, cool and shady forests, the Arctic Ocean, river sandbars, elevated gravel pads and raised road grades, and even the cool and shade under buildings on pillars at Prudhoe Bay.

If the environment does not provide insect-relief habitat, then the animals keep moving, at times running and stampeding. They often stand in dense clumps on hilltops with their heads down and together, hindquarters out. Apparently the simple obstructions of caribou bodies reduce attacks. Animals continually wheeze and shake to ward off insects.

The cool of early fall finally brings relief from summer's insect plagues.

Movements

In late winter, (anytime from March to early May) widely dispersed wintering groups of caribou begin to respond to an ancient call. As the days lengthen, they become increasingly restless. A few bands begin to move, meet and merge into increasingly greater aggregations moving toward their ancestral calving grounds. Some bands move north, others east, west or even south — it all depends on where they spent the winter in relation to the direction of their calving ground.

Toward these remote areas where their mothers gave birth to them, the pregnant cows trek so urgently in spring. Accompanied by yearling calves, the females march 15, 20, up to 40 miles each day, probably guided across this vast and seemingly featureless land by clues and memories retained from past migrations and from innate navigational abilities. The bulls have the luxury of following far behind at a more leisurely pace.

Once they reach the calving ground, the cows disperse. In the preceding fall, most females mated nearly at the same time, and now, in mid-June, most cows calve within a 10-day span. This reproductive synchrony has great

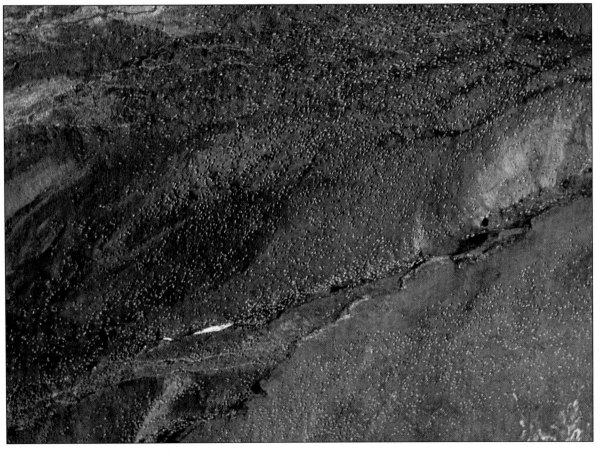

The Porcupine herd comes together in numbers too great to count during their post-calving aggregation. This herd has been subject to much study and publicity because its traditional migration route encompasses calving areas on the arctic coastal plain within the Arctic National Wildlife Refuge, an area much sought after by proponents of oil development, and the herd at times crosses the international boundary into Canada's Yukon Territory during movement from calving to wintering grounds. (James L. Davis)

survival value. Following the birth of the calves, the caribou begin to regroup. To caribou there is safety in numbers.

A tabular summary of the annual cycle of movements including associated degree of social aggregation and behavior appears in Table II, below.

Behavior

Like all living things, caribou are evolutionary products of their environment. Tom Bergerud noted in *Big Game of North America* in 1978 that major environmental factors that have molded the caribou include the weather (snow and wind), other animals (insects and wolves), visibility in the habitat (mostly open views for many populations) and the flora (slow-growing lichens). First, the open habitat plus the presence of wolves likely has fostered the caribou's gregarious

Table II: Annual cycle of caribou behavior and movements with associated viewing highlights.

TIME OF YEAR	PHASE OF THE ANNUAL CYCLE	RELATIVE DEGREE OF SOCIAL AGGREGATION (EXPECTED GROUP SIZE)	SPECIAL VIEWING HIGHLIGHTS
April-May	Spring migration	Highly aggregated (S0*1,000/group)	Long columns, light colored, long pelage; largest bulls with short but rapidly growing new velvet-antlers; cows with hard, polished antlers; body condition showing signs of winter
Late May-early June	Calving, calving pause	Scattered, cows often alone at birth (1-20 group)	Mother-offspring pairs, groups of cows and calves; cows lose antlers, motley pelage as winter coat shed; bulls becoming sleek, cows look thin
Late June-July	Postcalving aggregation, postcalving shift	Most aggregated of any time in the year (+ 10,000 group, some bulls and yearlings scattered)	Huge aggregations; caribou seeking relief from insects on snowbanks, gravel bars, sea and lake shores, windy ridges
August	Summer dispersal, summer shift	Very scattered (1-100, many singles)	Short, dark pelage, large velvet-covered antlers on bulls; beginning of fall colors
September	Fall shuffle, fall shift	Moderate aggregation (10-50 up to hundreds)	Peak fall colors; subsistence harvests; shed antler velvet; bulls and cows coming together; river crossings; sleek winter coats, long white neck manes; body condition good
October	Rut, fall pause	Highly aggregated (20-100 up to hundreds)	Sparring, fighting, courting, copulation; subsistence harvest
October-November	Fall migration	Highly aggregated long columns (up to many thousands/group)	Long columns, large numbers snow scenes
December-March	Winter pause	Widely scattered but local concentrations (10 to hundreds or thousands)	Cratering (pawing) in snow for food; bulls and cows segregated; bulls without antlers; wolf interactions

(Source: Alaska Department of Fish and Game, Fairbanks)

Jim Davis prepares an animal from the Nelchina herd for transport to the Kenai Peninsula in 1985. Both the Kenai Lowlands and Kenai Mountains herds began with transplants from other herds. (James L. Davis)

behavior. Grouping reduces predation, but precludes a sedentary mode of life because of the slow-growing flora and the variability of food supplies due to snow and wind. Thus, caribou became gregarious, but nomadic, denizens of the arctic prairies. Caribou move continuously, frequently in large groups. We might say caribou constantly move but pause periodically where an abundance of requisites occurs.

Habitat Needs and Preferences

For caribou two environmental needs stand out above all others: (1) to escape or find relief from flying insects in summer; and (2) to find food through deep snow in winter. These two needs greatly influence where caribou will be found. Some northernmost caribou populations comprise the only North American deer populations residing year-round north of the tree line.

In winter, caribou often seek areas of reduced snow cover or depth including south slopes and windswept mountains to locate food. These sites often have a limited absolute abundance of food, but because of reduced snow depths they offer high relative abundance.

Most people know of the caribou's affinity for "reindeer moss," which is actually lichen. However, most don't realize that caribou actually use a broad range of plants for food. Tom Bergerud wrote in 1978 that they eat a wider variety of plants than other deer species. He compiled a partial list of the plants eaten that included 62 lichens and 282 kinds of seed plants.

However, caribou show preference for green vascular plants and mushrooms. When these plants cannot be secured, caribou feed opportunistically, selecting any edible plants available.

In winter, in addition to eating lichens, caribou avidly dig for frozen green forage such as sedges and green leaves of evergreen shrubs. They also seek the fine twigs of birch, willow and blueberry. Under some conditions, caribou will shift from open habitats to forest cover seeking arboreal lichens growing on coniferous trees.

A cow in typical summer coat prances through the tundra of Denali National Park. A caribou's coat consists of long guard hairs that are thicker at the tip than at the base because they contain many air cells, and a fine underwool near the base of the guard hairs. Caribou can contract their skin to densely pack their hair, creating air bubbles near their skin. (Robin Brandt)

As spring advances, caribou quickly change their diet to include new vegetative growth. In mountainous regions, caribou seek new plant growth by shifting altitude and visiting receding snowfields. Grasses, sedges and cottongrass comprise the most important plant groups eaten here. The animals also seek other newly sprouting plants such as willow catkins, other shrubs and many forbs.

Green leaves of deciduous shrubs become the most important food in the summer diet, especially those of willow, shrub birch and blueberry. Caribou feed fastidiously, stripping leaves from woody stems and picking only new sprouts and finer stem tips. In late summer, they actively search for mushrooms.

Studies

Our knowledge of caribou has derived from many sources. Anecdotal knowledge and conventional wisdom continue to accrue from the many lay people who hunt, view, study and encounter caribou in their everyday activities.

The 15,000-year-old paintings of caribou left on the walls of caves in France by Cro-Magnon hunters attest to man's long interest in the caribou, as noted by George Calef in *Caribou and the Barren Lands* (1981). Calef offered a comprehensive summary of the studies that had been conducted prior to 1981. He noted that the written history of caribou in North America began with records of the arctic explorers. Martin Frobisher probably first saw and described caribou.

Early scientific studies such as those conducted by Olaus Murie in the 1930s in Alaska and adjacent Yukon and C.H.D. Clarke in Canada were hampered by the restricted means of travel available: dog team, canoe, snowshoes, skis and shanks mare. Obviously these means seriously limited anyone trying to keep up with the ever-moving caribou.

The difficulty of accurately estimating the number of caribou in vast tracts of wilderness also frustrated them. As Clarke commented with delightful irony, as late as the 1940s, "It is to be hoped that there will never be so few caribou that it will be possible to count them."

However, with advent of the bush plane, at last the uncountable could be counted.

Frank Banfield published his pioneering studies of the ecology of barren-ground caribou in Canada,

For several decades, scientists have been studying the effects of oil development on Alaska's North Slope environment, including its wildlife. While the long-term effects may not yet be known, it is apparent that some wildlife seem to go about their business, even with oil structures in their midst. (Larry Anderson)

which included the first aerial census of the major herds. Alaskans undertook similar surveys. Banfield also analyzed the taxonomy of caribou and reindeer, establishing the currently accepted subspecies.

Ronald Skoog produced a monumental thesis on the ecology of caribou in Alaska in 1968. John Kelsall the same year reported on the decade-long studies of barren-ground caribou by the Canadian Wildlife Service. These two works contain a comprehensive account on every aspect of caribou ecology and behavior.

More recent comprehensive accounts by individual authors include the book chapters written in 1978 and 1982 respectively by Tom Bergerud in *Big Game of North America* and Frank Miller in *Wild Mammals of North America*, and the entire book on caribou by George Calef mentioned above. A representative sample of the type of research that has been conducted and reported from 1970 to present appears in the Proceedings of North American Caribou Workshops and International Reindeer/Caribou Symposiums. One

or the other of these scientific meetings has been held every several years since 1972.

Future Of The Caribou

What does the future hold for North America's caribou? Two Canadian wildlife biologists, who have devoted much of their lives to the study and conservation of caribou, have offered contrasting views. Frank Miller wrote the following in 1982: "Currently I can see little cause for optimism, especially with regard to the future of migratory

Newborn calves are light brown or reddish brown with a darker stripe running along their back from their neck to their tail. Calves face a tough time their first year. In some herds in some years, less than five calves per 100 cows survive until fall. (James L. Davis)

concerted, all-out effort must be made — now. Federal, provincial, state, and territorial agencies charged with the responsibility for management and conservation of caribou and their ranges must vigorously press for the constraints necessary to protect the caribou."

In 1978 Tom Bergerud wrote the following: "In general, there is reason to be very hopeful for the future of caribou. They are highly adapted to their environment and also adaptable.... The ultimate question for caribou is the same as that once posed for bison — can the land be their's to wander."

Insufficient time has elapsed to test these two views. For now it looks like the odds are 50-50 that either view will prevail. Any reassurance for the caribou's long term well-being comes from current knowledge that suggests caribou can coexist with man if man will let them. ∎

herds of caribou. Subsistence users want to utilize the caribou beyond the maintenance capabilities of the herds. Exploitation of petroleum, gas, minerals, and water has the potential for disrupting migrations and reducing availability of caribou ranges. Politicians and pressure groups through misguided beliefs or lack of under-

standing or indifference are willing either to not act at all or to take the wrong actions on behalf of the caribou. Even some wildlife people suggest turning the management of caribou over to the native peoples-that indeed would not be a panacea for the caribou.

"If we are to manage and conserve caribou properly, a hitherto unknown,

Muskox

By Pam Groves

Editor's note: *Pam has worked with muskox since 1979 with the Musk Ox Development Corp. and the University of Alaska Fairbanks' Institute of Arctic Biology. She has a doctorate in wildlife biology and currently works as a research associate at the institute, studying genetic variabilities within muskoxen.*

With its shaggy, brown hair sweeping the ground and whitish re-curved horns, the muskox is a distinctive denizen of the Arctic. Muskox herds are well-known for forming a defensive circle with their hooked horns facing out when threatened by predators. This behavior and an insulating blanket of underwool are two of the adaptations that allow this fascinating species to survive the harsh environment of the Arctic, even on the northernmost land on the globe above 83 degrees latitude in northern Greenland.

With their thick winter coats, big shoulder humps and bushy manes of hair, muskoxen may appear to be larger than life. This is particularly apparent in photographs of these animals on the tundra where there are no trees or other objects to provide scale. Indeed, within its range, the muskox is usually the largest land mammal. At the southern extremes of their range, however, muskoxen may overlap with moose and in northern coastal areas with polar bears, both of which tend to be larger. Yet, muskoxen are surprisingly small. Mature males weigh up to about 800 pounds and stand up to 5 feet at the shoulder. Females tend to be a little smaller, weighing 500 to 600 pounds and measuring 4 feet at the shoulder. For comparison, North American bison, which muskoxen superficially resemble, can weigh up to 1 ton and stand 6 1/2 feet at the shoulder.

The long outer hairs that form the characteristic skirt on muskoxen are permanent guard hairs. This coarse brown hair continues to grow throughout the life of each animal. When muskoxen are born, the guard hairs are just an inch or two long. The hair grows slowly and not until animals are about 3 years old do they display the characteristic skirt of hair. In contrast, a new coat of underwool, known by the Eskimo name, *qiviut*, is grown and shed annually. The grayish-brown *qiviut* grows over the entire body to a depth of 6 inches and provides

FACING PAGE: *Muskox have fairly good eyesight. While they may not have sharp definition of objects within their view, they are able to pick out movement at some distance, an essential skill for detecting predators. (Lon E. Lauber)*

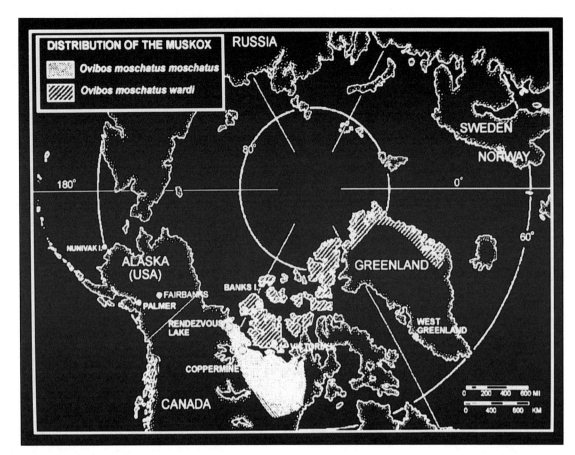

DISTRIBUTION OF THE MUSKOX
- *Ovibos moschatus moschatus*
- *Ovibos moschatus wardi*

excellent insulation against the cold of arctic winters. Adult muskoxen produce 5 to 7 pounds of *qiviut* each year. *Qiviut* is shed in the spring, rises to the surface of the guard hairs and falls to the ground. Pregnant cows do not shed until after they give birth and calves shed when about 6 to 8 weeks old. Some *qiviut* may become entangled in the long hair, particularly of the mane, and result in an unkempt and shaggy appearance. New *qiviut* begins to grow almost immediately, so by the onset of winter muskoxen are once again clad in winter coats.

Qiviut is a finer fiber than cashmere, the underwool of Asian goats. The soft fibers do not itch when placed against human skin and can be used to produce warm and beautiful garments. In the past, Native peoples of North America occasionally may have used *qiviut* to help keep themselves warm in winter, but it is only in recent decades that *qiviut* has been in demand as an exotic fiber for spinners, weavers and knitters.

Despite their unique coat, muskoxen share many physical characteristics with sheep, goats and cows. They all are ruminants with four-chambered stomachs and chew their cud to digest their herbivorous diet. All these animals have hooves with two toes, as opposed to the one-toed hooves of horses. Finally, all these animals have horns. Horns are distinct from the antlers of deer that are grown and shed each year. Barring serious injury, horns remain permanently attached to the head throughout the life of an animal.

Muskox calves begin growing horns during their first summer, but the horns do not reach full size until females are about 4 years old and males are 6 or 7 years old. For the first 2 to 3 years, the horns stick out to the side of the head. The horns of adult muskoxen drop down alongside the head and then curve up and outward to

a black-tipped hook. Horns of female muskoxen grow across the forehead and almost meet in the center. This part of the horn is small and often obscured by white hair. On males, these horn bases meet and thicken as the animals mature to form massive bosses 7 or 8 inches thick. During the mating season when males fight by engaging in a series of head-on clashes, this horn boss provides protection for the head.

Arctic Adaptations

The range of the muskox is limited to the Arctic and Subarctic. In this environment, muskoxen are usually found north of tree line on the tundra. Winters in this range are long and cold with little sunlight while summers are a short flush of sunshine and plant growth. Arctic environments tend to be arid without deep accumulations of snowfall. Often the snow that does fall is blown into drifts leaving much of the vegetation bare or with a thin blanket of snow. Thus while muskoxen have not evolved to survive in extensive, deep snow, they do possess adaptations to deal with the extreme climate, particularly cold, long winters.

Animals that live in the Arctic exhibit an assortment of strategies for survival. Many species, particularly birds, avoid arctic winters completely by migrating to southern regions. These animals take advantage of the intense arctic summers for breeding, feeding and raising their young and then leave. Caribou, the other arctic ungulate in addition to muskoxen, do not actually leave the Arctic during winter, but they do migrate between summer and winter feeding areas, frequently traveling long

Muskox cows bear their young between mid-April and June. Because snow usually remains well into spring throughout much of the muskoxen's range, calves are born with a layer of qiviut *and guard hair and have a supply of brown fat that can be used to produce heat. (Harry M. Walker)*

distances to obtain sufficient food resources. Other species, such as brown bears and arctic ground squirrels hibernate, and thus do not need to find food during winter. Some small arctic mammals stockpile food during summer and store it in caches for winter consumption. Some species that remain active during winter such as ptarmigan, lemmings, arctic hares, short-tailed weasels (ermines), least weasels and arctic fox change color to white in winter to blend in with their surroundings and avoid detection by predators or prey. Muskoxen employ none of the above strategies, but instead remain active within their home range throughout the year. To survive arctic winters, muskoxen have evolved a sedentary lifestyle that minimizes the amount of energy required to stay warm, find food and avoid predation.

The thick layer of insulating under-wool, or *qiviut*, is the most obvious adaptation to keeping warm in winter. The *qiviut* and guard hair hide other adaptations to the cold. Muskoxen do have tails, but they are only 2 inches long and remain hidden under the hair. A long tail exposed to the cold air would

Captive animals have only the sharp tips of their horns removed. The thick horn bosses on the forehead are left to provide important protection during head-butting clashes between fighting males. (Roy Corral)

be vulnerable to frostbite. Likewise, muskox ears are only 6 inches long and are completely covered with hair. During winter, the ears are buried in the long hair of the mane for further protection from the cold. Muskox legs, frequently obscured by the skirt of

guard hair, are short, stocky and covered with white hair and *qiviut* all the way down to the hoof. The hair extends down the face and nose with only the nostril edges and lips exposed.

Summer days in the Arctic where there are no trees for shade and the sun

FACING PAGE: *A muskox pair stand their ground in the Noatak Valley in April. Muskoxen disappeared from Alaska in the mid-1800s, but were reintroduced in the wild here in the 1930s. As the wild herd expanded, members of that herd were relocated to other areas in Alaska including the Seward Peninsula and Cape Thompson on the northwest coast. (Nick Jans)*

RIGHT: *This upper skull of a prehistoric muskox, the most complete specimen of this type in the University of Alaska Museum's collection, was unearthed in late 1996 by Ann Cunningham, a Fairbanks operating engineer. The skull was found about 50 feet down in a gravel pit, and according to Roland Gangloff of the university staff, the skull ranged in age from 25,000 to 100,000 years old. (Ben Grossman)*

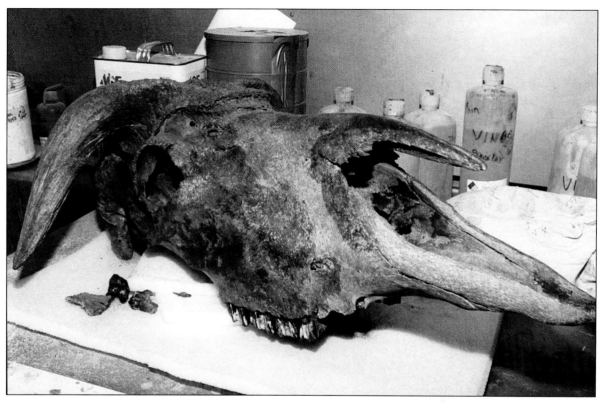

shines continuously can be surprisingly hot. At this time of year, the *qiviut* is growing and does not offer as much insulation as during winter. In addition, muskoxen avoid overheating on hot summer days by lying on snowbanks, standing in lakes or rivers and minimizing energy expenditure by moving only short distances. However, the muskox coat is still thick enough to provide protection from insect harassment that can be intense in summer. Caribou, which lack a thick coat, can be driven frantic by insects and will attempt to avoid them by endlessly moving. Thus, the thick coat

on muskoxen that appears to be primarily an adaptation against cold also provides benefits during summer.

The size of muskoxen confers several benefits for adapting to the Arctic. Within limits, a large-bodied animal, such as the muskox, has an improved ability to withstand extremely cold or hot temperatures because it has less surface area for its volume over which to lose or gain heat. The metabolic rate, or rate at which energy is used, of a large mammal is relatively lower than that of a small one so a muskox needs to consume relatively less food for its

body weight than a smaller animal. Additionally, larger animals can digest lower-quality food and thus may find overall food availability higher than that for smaller animals which must select for higher-quality food.

Indeed, muskoxen have been observed to be generalist feeders, consuming a variety of plants including grasses, sedges, forbs, herbs and shrubs. Muskox dietary preferences change during the course of the year depending on plant quality and availability. During the summer when plants are most easily available and of high quality, muskoxen can consume large quantities of food because of their large size. They are able to accumulate thick fat layers that provide both insulation and energy reserves for the winter. In winter, when plant quality declines, muskoxen are able to digest the lower-quality plants that remain available in windswept areas or areas where the accumulated snow can be scraped away by hooves.

An associated benefit of their relatively non-selective diet is that muskoxen do not need to move long distances while foraging to find appropriate food. In contrast to caribou, which move almost continuously while foraging, muskoxen are rather sedentary and will feed within a limited area for days at a time. The limited movement of foraging muskoxen results in reduced energy expenditure that is especially important in winter when energy conservation is crucial for survival. Because muskoxen can survive on a less-selective diet, they do not need to migrate between summer and winter feeding grounds as do caribou, further saving energy.

In addition to helping them stay warm and find adequate food, their large body size helps muskoxen avoid predation. The major predators of muskoxen are wolves as well as brown and polar bears, in some regions. When a group of muskoxen is threatened by a predator, they tend to run together, stand their ground and face the threat. If the threat is a pack of wolves surrounding them, the muskoxen form a circle with their heads facing outward and rumps and young animals protected in the center. Adult animals occasionally may charge out and attempt to attack the predator with their horn hooks by swinging their strong necks. Because of the potentially lethal horn hooks on both males and females, the defensive circle of muskoxen can be effective against predators. Predators are most successful hunting muskoxen if they can force the group to break and run so they can attack an animal from behind, away from the horns, or if they can surprise muskoxen and attack before the group can run together. This method of group defense is relatively uncommon in the animal world. It is commonly observed only among a few ungulate species such as the muskox, takin and African buffalo. All these

Muskox can run about 20 mph over short stretches, but seldom make prolonged runs because they are susceptible to overheating, even in winter. (Harry M. Walker)

species are large-bodied with stout horns, characteristics that appear to be critical for group defense to be effective in repulsing predators.

For muskoxen, group defense is interwoven with their other adaptations to life in the Arctic. Running a short distance to the group and standing to face a predator uses less energy than running long distances to escape from a predator, the method caribou frequently use to avoid predation. This conservation of energy is significant in the ability of muskoxen to survive arctic winters. Further, because of their thick insulation for winter, muskoxen are unable to run for such long distances as caribou. Their insulation is so effective in retaining body heat that muskoxen can overheat while running, even at winter temperatures well below freezing. Extreme overheating can be fatal or at least make an animal sick and more vulnerable to predation.

Because of their dependence on the group for defense from predators, muskoxen are social animals and tend to be uncomfortable when alone. Individuals that inadvertently become separated from the group show signs of panic and will call and run frantically until reunited with the

This mother watches closely as her calf, barely more than an hour old, tries to stand. (Pam Groves)

group. Groups, or herds, of muskoxen are normally composed of mixed age and sex animals. Males sometimes are observed singly, or in herds with no females, but it is extremely unusual to observe solitary females, or a herd of females with no males. Within each group, there is a definite hierarchy and dominant animals can readily displace subordinate ones from prime feeding locations. Surprisingly, large bulls show a remarkable tolerance for young playful calves that may run around and charge or even climb on a resting bull.

Group sizes of muskoxen do vary. Groups as large as 200 animals have been seen, although groups of less than 40 animals are more common. Groups also tend to be larger in winter than summer. Herd structure appears to be fluid with animals and subgroups joining and separating regularly. When two groups merge, some head butting and sparring may occur as the animals establish a new dominance hierarchy. Most herd movements appear to be spontaneous with no obvious leader. A group may remain in one small area for several days before moving one to

two miles to a new area to feed. Occasionally, when muskoxen travel longer distances, they may travel more or less in single file, apparently following the lead animal. Muskoxen normally remain within the same general area throughout the year. However, in rapidly expanding populations, dispersals of more than 200 miles have been documented as muskoxen move to colonize new ranges.

Life History

Muskox calves are born in spring, between mid-April and June. April, in the Arctic, is dominated by winter conditions with snow on the ground and cold temperatures, a seemingly harsh environment for a newborn animal. The calves, therefore, are born with a short layer of *qiviut* and guard hair to help insulate them against the cold. In addition, muskox calves are born with large reserves of brown fat, an energy-rich type of fat that can easily be burned to produce heat. The young calves lie touching their mothers for further protection from the cold.

Muskox cows normally give birth to just one calf at a time after a gestation of eight months. Because arctic summers are short, it is crucial for a cow to put her energy into producing adequate milk (up to more than half a gallon a day) for the one calf to grow large and strong enough during the summer to survive the following winter. Calves weigh about 20 to 25 pounds at birth and are small enough to stand under their mother's belly. These young calves can be completely hidden when under their mothers by her skirt of guard hair. Only their small white legs may be visible close to the ground. Muskox calves stand within an hour of birth, and although slightly wobbly are then able to follow their mothers. Newborn calves stay with their mothers throughout the day unlike many young ungulates that spend most of their time

lying hidden in the vegetation and only are visited by their mothers periodically to be nursed. Because muskox cows are capable of protecting their calves from predators and the tundra usually lacks appropriate vegetation for hiding calves, staying close by their mothers is safest for young muskoxen.

As the calves grow, they begin to venture away from their mothers and interact with each other. Like the young of many mammals, muskox calves are playful. Groups of calves will run in circles chasing each other and then turn and butt heads. They charge and butt inanimate objects as well as sleeping adults. A favorite calf game is "king of the mountain" in which calves will attempt to push one another off some small mound on the tundra. When a calf becomes hungry, it stops playing and bleats for its mother. The mother responds with a lionlike roar and the calf will run to her and dive under for a drink. Calves normally are weaned when they are 9 to 10 months old, although sometimes they will continue to nurse for more than a year.

Breeding season is in late summer, usually August. Prior to the peak of the season, females begin their estrous cycles that are about 20 days long and the males come into rut, or become sexually active. Muskoxen are harem breeders, which means a bull will attempt to gather a group of cows, guard them from other males and breed all the females in the group. To be able to gather and guard the females, a male must establish his dominance over other males. Therefore, rutting bulls spend much time posturing and fighting during this season. Rutting bulls tend to vocalize frequently, making a roaring sound, presumably to notify other bulls of their presence. The bulls rub a gland below their eye on their forelegs, dribble urine and horn and paw at the ground, possibly to distribute their scent around the area. When two rutting bulls meet, they strut around with a stiff-legged gait and arched necks. Preliminary to actually fighting, two bulls will face each other and slowly back up until they are up to 150 feet apart. After swinging their heads, the bulls charge full speed at each other and crash their horn bosses together. Following the forceful collision, they may shake their heads, then back up again and repeat the entire process. Sometimes a collision will be

A muskox harem roams the tundra of Canada's Banks Island. (Pam Groves)

followed by a head to head shoving match. A fight can continue for 10 or more collisions until one bull gives up and turns and runs away. The winning, dominant bull then returns to the harem. The massive horn boss on muskox bulls serves as a type of crash helmet and normally protects them from serious injury during a rutting fight.

When not occupied fighting challengers, a dominant bull spends his time keeping his harem rounded up and courting the cows. Cows only are receptive to a bull for a brief period during each estrous cycle. During this period, the bull will tend that cow closely and mount her as many times as she will stand for him. Muskox cows in good condition can conceive while they are still nursing a calf and thus can be pregnant and lactating simultaneously, producing a calf yearly. In areas where conditions are less favorable, cows often fail to give birth every year. Depending on their body condition, muskox cows can first conceive at 1 to 4 years of age. Bulls are sexually mature at 3 to 4 years of age, but usually are not large enough to win dominance fights and successfully breed cows until they are 5 to 6 years old.

A mature bull muskox (shown here) may weigh up to 800 pounds and reach 5 feet at the shoulder. A mature female weighs 500 to 600 pounds and stands 4 feet at the shoulder. (Lon E. Lauber)

Wild muskox cows have lived for more than 20 years, but a more common life expectancy for muskox cows is about 15 to 18 years. Because of the stress of rut, muskox bulls age more rapidly and tend to live about 10 to 12 years. In old muskoxen, the molars become worn down from years of cud chewing and the animals become less efficient at chewing and digesting their food. Some animals simply waste away, while others, weakened by poor nutrition, become victims of predation or extreme winter cold.

Relationships

With their pronounced shoulder humps, muskoxen are often mistakenly thought to be related to bison. Actually, muskoxen are more closely related to sheep and goats than to cattle and bison. Recent DNA studies suggest the closest relatives of the muskox to be an assemblage of rather obscure Asian species including the goral and serow as well as the North American mountain goat. Muskoxen are classified as belonging to the subfamily *Caprinae* within the family

Bovidae. This subfamily comprises animals more adapted to cold and mountainous climates than most cattle. In addition to the close relatives of the muskox, the *Caprinae* includes all sheep and goats, takin, a species once thought to be the closest relative of the muskox, and species such as saiga, chiru, tahr, aoudad, bharal and chamois.

Prehistory and History

Ancestors of the muskox are thought to have evolved in Asia. Central Asia was the center of evolution for all *Caprinae* during the Pliocene, about 2 to 7 million years ago. From Asia, muskox-type animals radiated west-ward into Europe and eastward, across the Bering Land Bridge to North America. Thus, for a time, prehistoric species of muskoxen had a vast distri-bution. However, about 10,000 years ago, at the end of the last glaciation, muskoxen disappeared from Europe and most of Asia. The last muskoxen in Siberia died off about 3,000 years ago, probably because of climatic changes.

Some of the early muskoxen in North America inhabited unglaciated areas of Alaska where, during the Pleistocene, about 2 million to 10,000 years ago, they roamed with mammoths and mastodons. Other of these prehistoric muskoxen wandered east and south. During the last glaciation, some of these animals retreated south in front of the advancing ice sheet. Fossil remains of prehistoric muskoxen have been found as far south as Texas and from the Pacific to Atlantic coasts. In the late Pleistocene, at the end of the glaciation, the global climate changed and altered the patterns of vegetation growing in different regions. Many animals, including mammoths and mastodons, were unable to adapt to the changes in types and amount of food and became extinct. Muskoxen, however, adapted by becoming smaller and contracting their range to the subarctic and arctic regions of North America. Descendants of these survivors are the modern muskoxen that comprise a single species known as *Ovibos moschatus.*

While muskoxen were obviously known to indigenous people who shared their range, the first published report of the species did not appear in Europe until 1720. This report, by a French officer stationed west of Hudson Bay described a species of cattle that smelled of musk and therefore was called *Boeufs-musquez* or musk cattle.

While muskoxen do not possess musk glands, this misnomer has persisted to the present in both the scientific and common names. In 1780, the muskox was introduced into the scientific literature as *Bos moschatus,* based on sketchy descriptions suggesting a type of cattle. By 1816, a new generic name, *Ovibos,* had been proposed to describe both the sheeplike (*Ovis*) and cattlelike (*Bos*) characteristics of the animal. Thus while indigenous northern people referred to it as *oomingmak* (various spellings are possible), which means "bearded one," the rest of the world officially recognizes this hairy animal as *Ovibos moschatus* or musky sheep/cattle.

Until the mid-1800s, *Ovibos moschatus* was distributed across northern Alaska, the Canadian mainland north of tree line, on most of the large islands in arctic Canada with the exception of Baffin Island and on the eastern and northern coasts of Greenland (see map page 58). Muskoxen, which were never numerous within Alaska, disappeared from the territory sometime during the mid-to late-1800s. There are no records of early European explorers and traders in Alaska actually seeing a live muskox, although some of these Europeans encountered Alaska Natives who had seen or heard of muskoxen. The demise of Alaska muskoxen was probably due largely to a natural decline caused by episodes

(continues on page 76)

Large Animal Research Station

By Kerre Martineau

University of Alaska Fairbanks' Large Animal Research Station (LARS) conducts regular studies on resident colonies of muskoxen, caribou and reindeer. LARS also maintains the first captive colony of caribou/reindeer hybrids.

LARS began as a facility to research muskoxen. The first colony was established with 16 muskoxen captured on Nunivak Island. Within a few years, caribou calves were transferred to the station from the Delta and Porcupine herds and colonies of reindeer and moose were also established. The moose colony has since been moved to the Alaska Department of Fish and Game Moose Research Center in Soldotna.

The station comprises 150 acres of pasture and boreal forest with on-site laboratories, offices and living quarters. University students, faculty, volunteers and visiting scientists participate in studies of the animals. Recent studies include endocrine and physiological controls, comparative nutritional and reproductive physiology, behavior and energetics, genetics and disease. The station also harvests and sells raw *qiviut* from the muskoxen each year. Sale of souvenirs and *qiviut* at the station help support its continuing operations.

Area high school students conduct studies on the animals with the help of graduate students and station workers. The university regularly offers field courses to give its undergraduate and graduate students an opportunity to work with the herds. Visitors can receive guided walking tours through the station during summer months, while platforms located along the perimeter of the station provide easy access for viewing the animals year-round. ●

LEFT: *Educational field trips are offered year-round for primary and secondary school children. They tour the grounds and learn about the history of the station and each of the animals. (Robin Brandt)*

FACING PAGE: *Activity cycles of muskoxen on different diets is observed and charted for use in the studies. Each animal has a different color paint mark so it can be easily identified from the observation towers. (Robin Brandt)*

TOP LEFT: *Summers can be unbearably hot for the thick-coated muskoxen, but Wendy, a young calf, finds cool refreshment at the water trough. (Susan M. Streaser)*

LEFT: *Young calves carry the same color identifier mark as their mothers indicating to researchers that they are an unseparated pair. (Susan M. Streaser)*

ABOVE: *Velvet from caribou and reindeer antlers is shed each year and sometimes ingested by the animals as a source of protein. On the Seward Peninsula, Koreans amputate the antlers of domestic reindeer and harvest the fresh velvet for medicinal purposes. (Susan M. Streaser)*

BELOW: *Since Alaska summers are short lived, grazing animals like muskoxen take advantage of fresh green grass when it is available. (Robin Brandt)*

RIGHT: *Station workers collect truckloads of lichens from around the Fairbanks area for their caribou and reindeer herds. Lichen, a favorite treat of caribou and reindeer, is often used as a bribe when trying to weigh in or examine the animals. (Susan M. Streaser)*

of extreme climatic variability such as heavy snow years or icing events that reduced food availability. The Native people in Alaska did hunt muskoxen, and when muskox numbers had already declined to low levels, this hunting may have contributed to the deaths of the last muskoxen indigenous to Alaska.

Muskoxen in Canada

The disappearance of muskoxen from Alaska coincided with dramatic declines of muskox populations elsewhere. During this period, muskoxen in Canada were being harvested for both their skins and meat. Trade in muskox hides was sponsored both by the Hudson's Bay Co. and American whaling ships that visited ports throughout arctic Canada. Muskox hides were in demand for carriage robes at the end of the 19th century, probably as a substitute for bison robes that became hard to obtain after bison were almost exterminated. As Europeans increased their presence in northern Canada, both as traders and explorers, they depended on the local fauna for food. With their rifles, they could easily slaughter entire herds of muskoxen and obtain enough meat to feed their crews as well as their numerous dog teams. However, on some of the remote islands of the Canadian archipelago where there was little or no hunting, muskox numbers also declined. This suggests that environmental factors also contributed to the decrease in muskoxen.

The dramatic decline in muskox numbers early this century generated concern that the species might be in danger of extinction. The Northwest

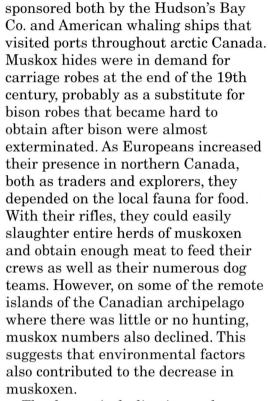

Calves from the Unalakleet herd forage among the shrubs of western Alaska. This herd was established with animals captured on Nunivak Island, transferred to Fairbanks where they were raised for 10 years, then relocated to Unalakleet. After several years at Unalakleet, the herd was moved once again, this time to Palmer in southcentral Alaska. (Pam Groves)

Game Act of 1917 granted protection from hunting to muskoxen in Canada. This original act provided an exception for Native peoples who needed meat to avoid starvation. When evidence accumulated that the exception was being abused, the act was amended in 1924 to totally prohibit hunting muskoxen. The hunting prohibition and termination of commercial exploitation of muskoxen was followed by a gradual increase of muskox numbers in Canada. In recent decades, many muskox populations have increased dramatically, particularly those on Banks and Victoria islands where almost two-thirds of Canadian muskox now live. The number of muskoxen in Canada is now estimated to be more than 145,000 animals and hunting quotas have been established for many populations.

Muskoxen in Alaska

Concern over the future survival of the muskox early this century generated an effort to reintroduce the species into Alaska. In 1930, the U.S. Congress appropriated $40,000 to purchase and transport muskoxen to the Territory of Alaska. That summer, 34 young muskoxen were captured in

A muskox skin hangs to dry at the Yup'ik community of Tununak on Nelson Island. Several of the herds in Alaska are hunted on a limited basis. (Harry M. Walker)

In most instances, the horns of a muskox remain with the animal throughout its life. Females produce full size horns by about age 4; males grow full-size horns by age 6 or 7. (Lon E. Lauber)

east Greenland and traveled by ship to New York via Norway. The animals spent one month in quarantine in New York and were then shipped by rail to Seattle. From Seattle, they again traveled by ship to Seward, Alaska and then again by rail to Fairbanks. Remarkably, all the animals survived this four-month epic journey.

The animals were held in captivity in large pastures at the University of Alaska at Fairbanks for five years while feeding and breeding studies were conducted. During this period, some animals were killed by local black bears. When funding for the research was terminated, the 31 surviving muskoxen were transported

to Nunivak, a 60- by 80-mile island, in the Bering Sea off the Yukon-Kuskokwim delta in western Alaska. This involved another trip by rail to Nenana and then by barge down the Tanana and Yukon rivers and across to Nunivak. While Nunivak is south of the historical range of indigenous Alaska muskoxen, it has no animal predators and had been established as a wildlife refuge, and so was thought to be an appropriate location for muskoxen.

Initially, the muskoxen increased in numbers slowly, but by 1968 the herd was estimated at more than 750 animals. Biologists became concerned muskoxen were overgrazing the vegetation and causing their environment to deteriorate. The Alaska Department of Fish and Game and the U.S. Fish and Wildlife Service initiated efforts to translocate muskoxen from Nunivak to other areas within Alaska. The first transplant was to Nelson Island adjacent to the mainland and near Nunivak in 1967. Between 1969 and 1981, groups of muskoxen were released on the Seward Peninsula and at Cape Thompson in northwest Alaska and in the Arctic National Wildlife Refuge in northeast Alaska.

Like their closest relatives, sheep, goats and cows, muskoxen have hooves with two toes. (Chlaus Lotscher)

Transplants to these last two areas reestablished muskoxen in their traditional range within Alaska.

After a period of little growth following each translocation, these populations became established and have increased. Annual rates of increase as high as 24 percent have been documented for some populations and have been associated with dispersal into new ranges. The muskoxen in northeast Alaska have expanded their range east into the Yukon and Northwest Territories of Canada and wandered south to the foothills of the Brooks Range. This population is currently estimated to number about 800 individuals. The Seward Peninsula population now numbers about 950 animals and the Cape Thompson population about 240 animals. Limited hunting is currently allowed of some of these populations. Hunting quotas have been established for the Nunivak and Nelson island muskoxen to attempt to maintain target populations of 500 and 250 animals respectively. The total number of muskoxen in Alaska is now close to 3,000.

Muskoxen in Greenland

Because of the remoteness of their range, muskoxen in Greenland were never heavily exploited by humans. In the late 19th century, Norwegian sealers working the northeast coast of Greenland did harvest muskoxen for meat and skins. A trade in live muskoxen also was established. The technique developed for live-capturing muskoxen entailed shooting all adults in a herd and then catching calves and yearlings, a rather gruesome approach from our modern perspective. Fortunately, captures of live muskoxen in recent decades have used techniques in which no animals are sacrificed. In total since 1899, about 300 live muskoxen have been removed from northeast Greenland.

Indigenous populations of muskoxen in north and northeast Greenland tend to increase during periods of favorable weather and decrease during adverse climatic trends. A small population of muskoxen in extreme northwest Greenland died out before the turn of the century. Because of the instability of

Greenlandic muskox populations and to fill presumed unoccupied niches as well as to add to the subsistence food base of Native people, muskoxen have been translocated within Greenland. Between 1962 and 1989, muskoxen have been translocated to areas of northwest, western and southwest Greenland. Subsistence hunting is permitted in areas where translocated muskoxen have become plentiful. In total, about 12,000 muskoxen now live in Greenland.

FACING PAGE: Besides their long flowing coat, muskoxen are likely most widely known for their unique defensive behavior. When threatened, muskoxen gather together with the young in the middle, and face outward toward the threat. This behavior forms an effective defensive perimeter that works well against most predators as long as the perimeter isn't broken by a bolting herd. (Lon E. Lauber)

RIGHT: Muskoxen have adapted in several ways to their arctic environment. To keep out cold and contain their body heat, muskoxen grow a dense coat of underwool called qiviut. *Their ears and short tail are shielded by long guard hairs and thick* qiviut. *Likewise, their short, stocky legs are protected by a skirt of long guard hairs and an insulating layer of* qiviut *growing all the way down to their hooves. (George Wuerthner)*

Translocations

Some efforts have been made to introduce muskoxen to regions that appear to offer suitable habitat but have no historical evidence of ever having been home to the species. Fossil evidence indicates muskoxen did inhabit regions of Siberia until about 3,000 years ago. In 1974-1975, 40 muskoxen from Nunivak Island and 10 from Banks Island, Canada,

were transported to Siberia. They were released into the wild on both the Taimyr Peninsula and Wrangel Island. These two populations now total 300 to 400 animals. The Ungava Peninsula of northern Quebec, Canada, has no known history of muskoxen, but resembles the habitat on the western shore of Hudson Bay, which has indigenous muskoxen. Thirteen muskoxen from Ellesmere Island,

Esther Shavings, originally from Mekoryuk on Nunivak Island, knits a garment with yarn made of qiviut. *Each knitter follows a pattern characteristic of her home village, in this case the harpoon pattern. (Harry M. Walker)*

for research at the University of Saskatchewan in Canada and the University of Tromso in Norway. Numerous zoos throughout the northern hemisphere have muskoxen on display and a few private individuals maintain small herds of muskoxen in captivity.

Subspecies

Presently, two subspecies of muskoxen are commonly recognized. These are the white-faced muskox, or *Ovibos moschatus wardi*, on Greenland and the arctic islands of Canada and the barren-ground muskox, or *Ovibos moschatus moschatus*, on the mainland of Canada. Subspecies are often defined as populations of a species that are morphologically distinct from each other and that do not interbreed, usually because of some geographic separation. Subspeciation of muskoxen has been proposed to have occurred during the Wisconsin glaciation (70,000 to 10,000 years ago) when white-faced muskoxen survived in refugia north of the ice while barren-ground muskoxen retreated south of the ice. As the ice melted, white-faced muskoxen could

Canada, were introduced to the Ungava Peninsula in 1967 as part of a domestication project. After domestication efforts ceased in 1972, the muskoxen were released into the wild in three separate groups. These populations have increased rapidly and now total more than 400 animals. Between 1947 and 1953, 27 muskoxen were translocated from northeast Greenland to the Dovre Mountains of Norway. This population has remained small at about 40 animals,

but a small group dispersed to Sweden and has maintained another small population there.

In addition to those in the wild, some muskoxen are maintained in captivity. Within Alaska, there are two captive muskox herds. One herd is in Palmer and is part of a domestication project in which muskoxen are raised for their *qiviut*. The University of Alaska has a research herd of muskoxen in Fairbanks. Captive herds of muskoxen also are maintained

Among the world's finest wool, qiviut *is warm, lightweight and doesn't scratch the skin. The wool is fashioned into scarves, hats, dresses, capes and other garments. (Danny Daniels)*

have dispersed throughout the arctic islands and to Greenland while barren-ground muskoxen moved north with the retreating ice edge to their present range.

White-faced muskoxen tend to have whiter faces and be smaller than muskoxen on the Canadian mainland. The two populations of muskoxen are theoretically separated by the barrier of water or ice between the mainland and the arctic islands. However, studies of proteins and DNA have found little variation among all muskoxen and have been unable to define any subspecific differences. Muskoxen are capable of dispersing over long distances and will travel over sea ice, so muskoxen may occasionally cross between the Canadian mainland and islands resulting in gene flow between the populations and reducing any genetic differences that may have evolved. Thus, it is possible that no valid subspecies of muskoxen exist.

The dramatic population fluctuations muskoxen have experienced repeatedly throughout time have probably caused genetic bottlenecks. A bottleneck occurs when a population is reduced to a few survivors and subsequently increases. The resulting population may contain many individuals, but the gene pool will be limited to the genes of the survivors. Repeated bottlenecks of muskoxen appear to have resulted in reduction of the overall genetic variability of the species. This lack of genetic variability is not necessarily detrimental to a wild species. For a species such as the muskox, the reduction in variability has occurred slowly during a period of many thousands of years. During this time, natural selection will have eliminated most deleterious genes from the gene pool. This contrasts with the inbreeding of domestic species that happens during a short time and where natural selection does not have the opportunity to rid the populations of unhealthy genes. Consequently muskox populations, even those founded by a small number of individuals, can be healthy and thriving in their current environment. However, lack of genetic variability can reduce the genetic plasticity of a species rendering it more vulnerable to any changes in the environment. With predictions of global change and increasing human activity in the Arctic, there should be concern that muskoxen may lack the genetic variability to adapt to these changes.

Viewing Muskoxen in Alaska

Viewing wild muskoxen in Alaska is likely to be expensive and not guaranteed. Muskoxen can occasionally be sighted from the Dalton Highway north of the Brooks Range. The Dalton is the highway built as the haul road for the trans-Alaska pipeline and is connected to the main Alaska road system. However, it is a long drive over a rugged road, and muskoxen may not be visible. Muskoxen are being sighted with increasing frequency off roads around Nome on the Seward Peninsula. Nome is only accessible by air from the rest of Alaska. Likewise, the other wild populations of muskoxen in the state are only accessible by air and then usually by small plane, helicopter, boat, snow machine, all-terrain vehicle or foot.

The best opportunities for viewing muskoxen at a close distance are at the three locations in the state with captive muskoxen. The Alaska Zoo in south Anchorage has a display with muskoxen. Larger herds of muskoxen can be viewed at the Musk Ox Farm in Palmer and the Large Animal Research Station in Fairbanks.

The Musk Ox Farm in Palmer is owned and operated by the Musk Ox Development Corp. This muskox herd was established with young muskoxen captured on Nunivak Island in 1964 and 1965 as part of a domestication project that was the result of an initiative by John J. Teal. It is the oldest captive muskox herd in existence. The herd was kept in Fairbanks for a decade and was then transferred to Unalakleet on the west coast for another decade and has finally settled in Palmer. These animals are raised for their *qiviut*, which is used to supply a knitting cooperative composed of Native Alaska women. This cooperative, Oomingmak, the Musk Ox Producers' Co-operative, has headquarters in Anchorage.

LEFT: *In summer, muskoxen can be found standing in water to cool off. (Harry M. Walker)*

FACING PAGE: *Descendants of a widely distributed prehistoric ancestor, muskoxen found in present-day Alaska all come from a group of 34 animals captured in east Greenland in 1930. (Harry M. Walker)*

Emphasis is placed on raising tame animals that can be intensively handled. The Musk Ox Farm is open for public tours daily throughout summer and provides an opportunity for close viewing of muskoxen.

The Institute of Arctic Biology, part of the University of Alaska Fairbanks, operates the Large Animal Research Station on Yankovich Road. The station maintains captive muskoxen, reindeer and caribou. The muskox herd was started in 1979 with animals captured on Nunivak Island. Research at the station has focused on aspects of behavior, growth, nutrition, reproduction and metabolism of muskoxen in an attempt to better understand their adaptations to life in the Arctic. Results of this research can be used by wildlife biologists to better manage the wild muskox herds. During summer, tours of the station are available on Tuesdays, Thursdays

To rafters traveling North Slope rivers, cavorting muskoxen are reminiscent of mops rocking across the tundra. This herd was photographed in the Canning River valley of the Arctic National Wildlife Refuge. (George Wuerthner)

and Saturdays. At other times, muskoxen can frequently be observed from the viewing platforms by the parking lot on Yankovich Road. ■

By Kerre Martineau

Editor's note: *Kerre is a journalism student at University of Alaska Anchorage and editorial assistant with ALASKA GEOGRAPHIC®.*

I buried my hands in her thick coat of long coarse outer hairs and felt the soft *qiviut* underneath. This warm, dense layer was an impenetrable shield protecting her skin.

Siniq seemed to enjoy the attention. She's grown

Muskoxen are most content to remain outside at all times. The animals are only in the barn for brief periods when being weighed or combed. Most of the barn is used for tourist information and the gift shop. (Steve McCutcheon)

The Musk Ox Farm

accustomed to life on the farm and regular visitors. She and the rest of the Palmer herd appeared content roaming the fields on their 75-acre farm. They remain outside all year, their *qiviut* providing insulation from winter winds and freezing temperatures. Each spring when the temperature warms, farm workers comb and harvest the *qiviut,* which eventually is fashioned into garments for sale in Alaska stores. These items are in high demand because of their rarity and warmth. Found only on muskoxen, *qiviut* is eight times warmer than sheep's wool and finer than cashmere.

Oomingmak, the Musk Ox Producers' Co-operative in downtown Anchorage organizes the *qiviut*-knitting production. Raw wool is purchased from the farm, sent to a cashmere company where it is spun into fine yarn, and distributed to co-op members to knit various articles for sale. Currently, more than 200 women from 12 areas participate in this cottage industry.

Each participating area has a signature pattern that is woven into articles

LEFT: *Calves are born in early spring and nurse throughout the summer to gain required nutrients to survive their first winter. (Danny Daniels)*

TOP RIGHT: *Diane Rose, tourism director, displays a new* qiviut *scarf that has been washed and blocked to shape it for packaging and sale. The scarf shows a butterfly pattern, the signature design for Bethel knitters. (Kerre Martineau)*

RIGHT: *Nellie Forbes of Wainwright knits a scarf to be sold at the co-op.* Qiviut *used by co-op members is never dyed; all garments are finished in the orginal ash-brown color of the wool. (Chris Arend, courtesy of Oomingmak)*

produced by its knitters. These patterns are related to some unique feature of that particular area. For example, the butterfly design Bethel incorporates is derived from the pattern on parka trims worn there. Sometimes subtle, the patterns allow for identification of the village of origin of each piece.

Most knitters either learn their trade from their mothers or grandmothers or from one of the grant-sponsored workshops held in the villages. Some who attended the first teaching workshop in 1968 are still working members today. Each knitter sets her own schedule and can work as often or as little as she likes. When she finishes a piece, she sends it to the Anchorage office where the article is washed, blocked, labeled and packaged for sale. Knitters are paid for the pieces they produce and also receive a share of the year-end profit from sales. Overall, the co-op produces 3,000 to 4,000 items per year and sells all that they produce. Currently, co-op members can be found in Bethel, Unalakleet, Quinhagak, Tununak, Nightmute, Newtok, Toksook Bay, St. Mary's, Marshall, Mekoryuk, on the Seward Peninsula and on the Aleutians.

John Teal originated the idea for the farm in 1954.

He wanted a way for Alaska Natives to supplement their subsistence lifestyle using an animal indigenous to Alaska. After 10 years of intensive research on the muskoxen and their wool, the captures began. Through the assistance of the University of Alaska Fairbanks and a grant from the Kellogg Foundation, muskoxen were captured on Nunivak Island and spent 10 years at the university. From there the herd was moved to Unalakleet, but this proved to be too remote for supplies and proper veterinary care for the animals and in another 10 years they were relocated to Palmer.

Teal's son, Lansing, now manages the farm and is executive director for the Musk Ox Development Corp., which oversees the project. The farm is a year-round operation focused on the maintenance and

In 1968, the first workshop to teach Alaska Native women the knitting process was held on Nunivak Island, where the original muskoxen were captured. (Courtesy of Oomingmak)

A new layer of qiviut *begins to grow as soon as shedding starts. The long outer hairs are not shed; they continue to grow for the life of the muskox. (Steve McCutcheon)*

again moved to separate fields. In February, an ultrasound is performed on all harem females to determine which are pregnant. Pregnant females are then monitored every four hours to ensure the calf's safety and health until they give birth in the spring. Calves are born with a coat of *qiviut* to insulate them in their first months. The mothers begin shedding their *qiviut* as soon as they give birth, so the combing process begins.

Muskoxen are intelligent creatures and quickly learn the farm routine. Many enjoy the attention they receive during the combing process, but some prefer to stay away from the barn and stalls. Combing takes approximately two hours to complete on an adult muskox. Every inch of their coat must be combed to harvest as much *qiviut* as possible. The combing stalls are just big enough for one animal and one person so the comber can stand behind the animal's head without fear of being injured by its horns should the animal become anxious or aggressive. To minimize potential harm for the workers and increase handling ability, the horns are removed from non-breeding animals. The sharp tips of the horns are cut off many of the others.

For efficiency and safety, the farm is divided into multiple sections. The front field is designated for young calves, their mothers, and surrogate mothers who fill in as caretakers of the calves when needed. Another field houses older bulls and steers (castrated males that are dehorned and kept for their wool production). When not in a harem, the females also have a field of their own. Young bulls are the exception to the division of land. While they are separated from most of the other animals, they have a baby sitter in their midst. Nineteen-year-old Burt is the oldest of the Palmer herd and resides with the 2- to 3-year-old

proliferation of the woolly animals. Each fall, during rutting season, muskoxen are selectively bred by grouping a single male with a small harem of females in a separate back pasture for two months. Once the females are out of their estrous cycles, they are once

Lansing Teal, manager of the Musk Ox Farm, supervises the care of the animals and provides constant human contact, an important element in the domestication process. (Kerre Martineau)

bulls. He is too old to withstand the constant head-butting dominance fights of the other mature bulls and his wise demeanor helps to calm the younger animals.

As a non-profit organization, the Musk Ox Development Corp. relies on donations and grants to keep all the animals healthy and productive. Each year the farm receives numerous requests from students, mostly veterinary majors, wanting to work as interns with the animals. Many volunteers donate their time combing and feeding the muskoxen and performing general farm duties. Various levels of involvement are available to any member of the public wishing to donate through Friends of the Musk Ox, an organization for those interested in helping the muskox project.

Revenue from tours and

the on-site gift shop also provide much needed income. Tourists from all corners of the world visit Alaska and the Musk Ox Farm is frequently on their itinerary. The farm opens to tourists on Mother's Day and runs through September with tours given regularly throughout the day. Any given summer day can see 300 to 400 visitors at the

farm. To keep up with the influx of tourists, up to 13 tour guides are hired to explain the details of the muskox, the farm and the *qiviut*. Diane Rose, tourism director, began working at the farm in 1987 as a tour guide and now is charged with all advertising and publicity projects. She works year-round to manage and organize the visitor services

and ensures that each new guide is trained and prepared for the four-and-a-half month tourist season.

To tourists and unfamiliar visitors, the animals all look alike: large, brown, moplike creatures with stubby legs, long hair and curled horns. But walking among them, it is easy to see that each is unique in some way (besides its numbered ear tag).

Many in the herd have white faces. This distinction is from their Greenland heritage. The Greenland breed is slightly smaller than the more common Canadian muskox with its solid brown face. Through selective breeding, the farm is experimenting with cross-breeding the Greenland with the Canadian to determine if the combination has any impact on the animal's wool production. Another unique feature about each of them is their names. Joe Montana, Gilda, Samson, Bo and of course old Burt are just a sample of the names given to the animals. Certainly their personalities distinguish them from one another also. Some shy away from visitors while others approach curiously. All of them recognize Lansing and he automatically knows which ones want their bellies scratched, which prefer not to be touched on their heads, and which are a little aggressive with their horns.

These animals appear quite content in their domestic lives. Longer life spans, regular food and positive attention are all benefits of life on the farm. During the summer they can be seen romping through their fields, playing with their giant tether balls, fighting over back scratches from the automatic car wash brushes donated by local supporters, or just sleeping in the sun. Winter is quiet, no tourists to watch and out of reach of predators. Of course, the benefit to the people of Alaska is even greater. Village workers have the chance to preserve one of Alaska's indigenous mammals and work in harmony with them to produce items of great public demand. A knitter, a needle and a muskox equal the potential for perpetual work and income in the bush villages of Alaska. ●

LEFT: *Domestic muskoxen do not need to forage for winter foods buried in the snow as do their wild cousins. Instead, they are provided with a regular diet of hay and grains year-round. (Kerre Martineau)*

FACING PAGE: *In the spring,* qiviut *begins to shed and rises to the surface of the long outer hairs making it easy for combers to peel it off in layers during the annual combing process. An adult muskox will shed up to 6 pounds of* qiviut *each year, enough wool for more than 50 scarves. (Danny Daniels)*

Bibliography

Index

Allen, J. "Ontogenetic and other variations in muskoxen, with a systematic review of the muskox group, recent and extinct." *Memoirs of the American Museum of Natural History, New Series*, 1:101-226, 1913.

Banfield, A.W. Frank. *A Revision of the Reindeer and Caribou, Genus Rangifer*. National Museums of Canada, Biological Series 66, Bulletin 177, 1961.

Barr, W. *Back from the Brink*. Calgary: Arctic Institute of North America, 1991.

Bergerud, A. Tom. "Caribou" pp. 83-101 in *Big Game of North America*. Harrisburg, PA: Stackpole Books, 1978.

Bruemmer, Fred. *Arctic Animals*. Ashland, WI: NorthWord Inc., 1986.

Burch, E. S. "Muskox and man in the central Canadian subarctic, 1689-1974." *Arctic*, 30:135-154, 1977.

Calef, George W. *Caribou and the Barren-lands*. Ottawa: Canadian Arctic Resources Committee; Toronto: Firefly Books Limited, 1981.

Gray, D. R. *The Muskoxen of Polar Bear Pass*. Markham, Ontario: Fitzhenry and Whiteside, 1987.

Groves, P. *Muskox Husbandry*. Special Report No. 5, Biological Papers. Fairbanks: University of Alaska, 1992.

Harington, C. R. *History, distribution and ecology of the muskoxen*. M.S. Thesis, Montreal: McGill University, 1961.

Holst, B. *International Studbook for Muskox, Ovibos moschatus*. Copenhagen, Denmark: Copenhagen Zoo, 1990.

Hone, E. *The Present Status of the Muskox in Arctic North America and Greenland*. Philadelphia: American Committee for International Wildlife Protection, Special Publication No. 5, 1934.

Kelsall, John P. *The Migratory Barren-ground Caribou of Canada*. Ottawa: Queen's Printer, 1968.

Klein, D. "The establishment of muskox populations by translocation." in *Translocations of Wild Animals*, L. Nielson and R. Brown, eds. Wisconsin Humane Society & Kingsville, TX.: Kleberg Wildlife Research Institute, 1988.

Klein, D., R. White, and S. Keller. *Proceedings of the First International Muskox Symposium*. Special Report No. 4, Biological Papers. Fairbanks: University of Alaska, 1984.

Lent, P. "Ovibos moschatus." *Mammalian Species*, Provo, UT: American Society of Mammalogists, 302:1-9, 1988.

Miller, Frank L. "Caribou (*Rangifer tarandus*)" pp. 923-959 in *Wild Mammals of North America*. Baltimore, MD: Johns Hopkins University Press, 1982.

Skoog, Ronald O. *Ecology of the Caribou (Rangifer tarandus granti) in Alaska*. Ph.D. Thesis. Berkeley: University of California, 1968.

Teal, J. "Domesticating the wild and woolly muskox." Washington, D.C.: National Geographic, 137:862-878, 1970.

Tener, J. *Muskoxen in Canada: A Biological and Taxonomic Review*. Ottawa: Queen's Printer, 1965.

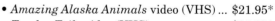

ALASKA GEOGRAPHIC. Back Issues

The North Slope, Vol. 1, No. 1. Out of print.

One Man's Wilderness, Vol. 1, No. 2. Out of print.

Admiralty...Island in Contention, Vol. 1, No. 3. $19.95.

Fisheries of the North Pacific, Vol. 1, No. 4. Out of print.

Alaska-Yukon Wild Flowers, Vol. 2, No. 1. Out of print.

Richard Harrington's Yukon, Vol. 2, No. 2. Out of print.

Prince William Sound, Vol. 2, No. 3. Out of print.

Yakutat: The Turbulent Crescent, Vol. 2, No. 4. Out of print.

Glacier Bay: Old Ice, New Land, Vol. 3, No. 1. Out of print.

The Land: Eye of the Storm, Vol. 3, No. 2. Out of print.

Richard Harrington's Antarctic, Vol. 3, No. 3. $19.95.

The Silver Years, Vol. 3, No. 4. $19.95.

Alaska's Volcanoes, Vol. 4, No. 1. Out of print.

The Brooks Range, Vol. 4, No. 2. Out of print.

Kodiak: Island of Change, Vol. 4, No. 3. Out of print.

Wilderness Proposals, Vol. 4, No. 4. Out of print.

Cook Inlet Country, Vol. 5, No. 1. Out of print.

Southeast: Alaska's Panhandle, Vol. 5, No. 2. Out of print.

Bristol Bay Basin, Vol. 5, No. 3. Out of print.

Alaska Whales and Whaling, Vol. 5, No. 4. $19.95.

Yukon-Kuskokwim Delta, Vol. 6, No. 1. Out of print.

Aurora Borealis, Vol. 6, No. 2. $19.95.

Alaska's Native People, Vol. 6, No. 3. $24.95.
LIMITED SUPPLY

The Stikine River, Vol. 6, No. 4. $19.95.

Alaska's Great Interior, Vol. 7, No. 1. $19.95.

Photographic Geography of Alaska, Vol. 7, No. 2. Out of print.

The Aleutians, Vol. 7, No. 3. Out of print.

Klondike Lost, Vol. 7, No. 4. Out of print.

Wrangell-Saint Elias, Vol. 8, No. 1. Out of print.

Alaska Mammals, Vol. 8, No. 2. Out of print.

The Kotzebue Basin, Vol. 8, No. 3. Out of print.

Alaska National Interest Lands, Vol. 8, No. 4. $19.95.

Alaska's Glaciers, Vol. 9, No. 1. Revised 1993. $19.95.

Sitka and Its Ocean/Island World, Vol. 9, No. 2. Out of print.

Islands of the Seals: The Pribilofs, Vol. 9, No. 3. $19.95.

Alaska's Oil/Gas & Minerals Industry, Vol. 9, No. 4. $19.95.

Adventure Roads North, Vol. 10, No. 1. $19.95.

Anchorage and the Cook Inlet Basin, Vol. 10, No. 2. $19.95.

Alaska's Salmon Fisheries, Vol. 10, No. 3. $19.95.

Up the Koyukuk, Vol. 10, No. 4. $19.95.

Nome: City of the Golden Beaches, Vol. 11, No. 1. $19.95.

Alaska's Farms and Gardens, Vol. 11, No. 2. $19.95.

Chilkat River Valley, Vol. 11, No. 3. $19.95.

Alaska Steam, Vol. 11, No. 4. $19.95.

Northwest Territories, Vol. 12, No. 1. $19.95.

Alaska's Forest Resources, Vol. 12, No. 2. $19.95.

Alaska Native Arts and Crafts, Vol. 12, No. 3. $24.95.

Our Arctic Year, Vol. 12, No. 4. $19.95.

Where Mountains Meet the Sea, Vol. 13, No. 1. $19.95.

Backcountry Alaska, Vol. 13, No. 2. $19.95.

British Columbia's Coast, Vol. 13, No. 3. $19.95.

Lake Clark/Lake Iliamna, Vol. 13, No. 4. Out of print.

Dogs of the North, Vol. 14, No. 1. $19.95. LIMITED SUPPLY

South/Southeast Alaska, Vol. 14, No. 2. Out of print.

Alaska's Seward Peninsula, Vol. 14, No. 3. $19.95.

The Upper Yukon Basin, Vol. 14, No. 4. $19.95.

Glacier Bay: Icy Wilderness, Vol. 15, No. 1. Out of print.

Dawson City, Vol. 15, No. 2. $19.95.

Denali, Vol. 15, No. 3. $19.95.

The Kuskokwim River, Vol. 15, No. 4. $19.95.

Katmai Country, Vol. 16, No. 1. $19.95.

North Slope Now, Vol. 16, No. 2. $19.95.

The Tanana Basin, Vol. 16, No. 3. $19.95.

The Copper Trail, Vol. 16, No. 4. $19.95.

The Nushagak Basin, Vol. 17, No. 1. $19.95.

Juneau, Vol. 17, No. 2. Out of print.

The Middle Yukon River, Vol. 17, No. 3. $19.95.

The Lower Yukon River, Vol. 17, No. 4. $19.95.

Alaska's Weather, Vol. 18, No. 1. $19.95.

Alaska's Volcanoes, Vol. 18, No. 2. $19.95.

Admiralty Island: Fortress of Bears, Vol. 18, No. 3. $19.95.
LIMITED SUPPLY

Unalaska/Dutch Harbor, Vol. 18, No. 4. $19.95.

Skagway: A Legacy of Gold, Vol. 19, No. 1. $19.95.

ALASKA: The Great Land, Vol. 19, No. 2. $19.95.

Kodiak, Vol. 19, No. 3. $19.95.

Alaska's Railroads, Vol. 19, No. 4. $19.95.

Prince William Sound, Vol. 20, No. 1. $19.95.

Southeast Alaska, Vol. 20, No. 2. $19.95.

Arctic National Wildlife Refuge, Vol. 20, No. 3. $19.95.

Alaska's Bears, Vol. 20, No. 4. $19.95.

The Alaska Peninsula, Vol. 21, No. 1. $19.95.

The Kenai Peninsula, Vol. 21, No. 2. $19.95.

People of Alaska, Vol. 21, No. 3. $19.95.

Prehistoric Alaska, Vol. 21, No. 4. $19.95.

Fairbanks, Vol. 22, No. 1. $19.95.

The Aleutian Islands, Vol. 22, No. 2. $19.95.

Rich Earth: Alaska's Mineral Industry, Vol. 22, No. 3. $19.95.

World War II in Alaska, Vol. 22, No. 4. $19.95.

Anchorage, Vol. 23, No. 1. $21.95.

Native Cultures in Alaska, Vol. 23, No. 2. $19.95.

The Brooks Range, Vol. 23, No. 3. $19.95.

PRICES AND AVAILABILITY SUBJECT TO CHANGE

Membership in The Alaska Geographic Society includes a subscription to *ALASKA GEOGRAPHIC®*, the Society's colorful, award-winning quarterly.

Call or write for membership rates or to request a free catalog. *ALASKA GEOGRAPHIC®* back issues are also available (see above list). **NOTE:** This list was current in early 1997. If more than a year or two have elapsed since that time, <u>please contact us to check prices and availability of back issues</u>.

When ordering back issues please add $2 postage/handling per book for Book Rate; $4 each for Priority Mail. Inquire for non-U.S. postage rates. To order send check or money order (U.S. funds only) or VISA/MasterCard information (including expiration date and your phone number) with list of titles desired to:

ALASKA GEOGRAPHIC.
P.O. Box 93370 • Anchorage, AK 99509-3370
Phone: (907) 562-0164 • Fax (907) 562-0479

NEXT ISSUE:

Alaska's Southern Panhandle

Vol. 24, No. 1. Led by Ketchikan, which likes to call itself "The First City," Southern Southeast is usually the first area of the state seen by visitors traveling north by water from the country's west coast. The area has a rich history of powerful Native groups, pioneering fish canneries and commercial fishing fleets, an important timber industry and a thriving tourist industry. To members mid-1997.